On the Road Home

A Sequel to Tangled Roots

EUNICE LONG

authorHOUSE®

AuthorHouse™
1663 Liberty Drive
Bloomington, IN 47403
www.authorhouse.com
Phone: 1-800-839-8640

First published by AuthorHouse   7/19/2010

ISBN: 978-1-4520-4867-3 (e)
ISBN: 978-1-4520-4866-6 (sc)

Library of Congress Control Number: 2010909840

Printed in the United States of America
Bloomington, Indiana

This book is printed on acid-free paper.

Dedication

I dedicate this book to my husband, Bill who has, as usual, given me his whole heartily support. His patients and understanding has been a great asset to me. To my son, Eddie who has been very helpful with his computer expertise, photography, and typing, a big thank you. In memory of my only daughter, Linda, who always encouraged me with her love and consideration. To my sister, Jo, who kept pushing me forward, and helping with the proof reading. To my granddaughters, Brandi and Shellee. Your lasting love keeps me smiling. Now last, but not least, to my dear friend Tonya. Your love and support is greatly appreciated. Thank you.

Chapter 1

Jody was the tallest boy in his high school classes, and he was very proud of that. He made good grades, and stayed on the honor-roll. He left girls alone, as his mother taught him to do. His biggest problem was what he wanted to become. He has enough confidence in himself to become whatever he wished, but what? His mother encouraged him with her positive attitude and determination, but she would not tell him in what direction to start out. She would support his decisions and the finances needed to accomplish his goal. Time was running out. Jody graduated still standing at the cross road. "You can't ring a goal if you don't have one." Maria told him.

Easter was around the corner, and the family members were coming for a reunion. Everyone would be asking the same question. "What are you going to do?" Jody felt like running away, but he wanted to see his grandparents. If he went off to college, it would be a long time before he could see then again. He particularly wanted to see his grandfather. He could talk with him and ask him questions. Paps could come up with answers. Jody knew his grandfather was a smart and brilliant man. Paps knew how to solve problems. Yes, a final decision was about to take place.

While every one was cooking, serving, cleaning, or running and screaming, Jody and his Paps sit down for a chat. His Paps had been a medical doctor, and Jody was beginning to think about that road. "If you decide to become a medical doctor, I will support you all the way. It's a good field to get into. It requires hard work, but you can handle that. You will need to move into a highly populated area. Don't do as I did and stay in a small community where you want make any money— well not much anyway. Doctors today can become millionaires." Paps smiled. Jody whispered, "I don't know if Mom has enough money." Paps replied, "Yes, she does. What did I just tell you? There is someone who can and will help you as far as you want to go." Jody placed his arms around Paps and gave him a big hug.

Jody relaxed and began to mingle with other family members. He felt so relieved. He now knew what he was going to do. Paps went and placed his arms around Maria, Jody's mother, who was also Pap's daughter. He pulled her close to him and whispered, "Everything will be alright. Look at him over there laughing and talking. He's made a decision, and you are going to love it. You're going to miss him, but he will be alright. What about me buying him a small car tomorrow? He will need his own vehicle to leave in." Maria placed her hands over her face and began to cry. She nodded her head as an O.K. to her Dad. He placed his arms around her shoulders and guided her to the back porch.

At the car lot, Jody could not find a vehicle that he could choose. He wanted all of them. He couldn't decide on color or model, perhaps a truck, or a van, maybe a convertible. Paps was getting tired of walking all over the car lot again and again. "Alright." Paps said. "You seem to like a truck, so choose one." "What about that red four door?" Jody asked. Paps said, "The one I'm pointing to is that red two door. You don't need a four door." Jody walked up to the truck. "This one!" He said. And that was the one he drove home.

"Maybe we all should plan to move on. Nobody cares about the farm any more. I have someone who wants to buy it. Let's all follow Jody. What do you think?" Paps asked Maria. Her reply was, "Have you talked with Mom about this?" "Yes. I have, and she is ready for a move." After everyone had left that night, Jody sat down with his mother and grandparents. Paps brought up the idea of the move. Jody jumped up and down. "Then, I'll still be near the family. Mom, you and Paps might get a job at the V.A. Hospital. It's right there next to the Medical College." They both laughed and said "Perhaps."

Moving three hundred miles from home to start a new life was not easy, but it turned out to be the very best choice they could have made. The four of them together, and living next door to each other, gave them a quiet peace. The neighborhood was very pretty. And the neighbors they'd met, seemed very nice. Finding a new church was a problem. At the farm, there was only one. But here there were ten or twelve Baptist Churches. How does one make a choice among so many? They tried them all, and then chose one. After meeting many families, going out to lunch together, and really enjoying the minister, they began to fit into the congregation, and feel at home. Since Jody was brought up in the church, he was excited they had found one.

There was a state park in the area, a skating rink, and a bowling alley. There was a large two-story mall, and most anything else one might be interested in. Jody was awed at all the shopping options available to him. While his Mon and Granny shopped, he and Paps drove all over the area. Jody wanted to learn his way around. He drove all over the college campus. He knew he had to learn his way through and around the campus. Paps also enjoyed the rides and the views. They took a good look through the park. Surely, they would come there often. There were massive picnic shelters, picnic tables scattered all around, and even restrooms. Jody observed. "Paps, this is where we will picnic and have our family reunions." They saw a sign directing traffic to the zoo. Jody was awed. He had never seen a zoo. He immediately turned into the zoo territory. The zoo is all that anyone could speak of at the dinner table that night. Jody wanted his Mom and Granny to go there. They set a date that all four of them would go.

Maria had noticed something different taking place in Jody's inner being. Some days he would come home from college all excited, laughing and talking about two or three subjects at the same time. Other days he was too quiet, in deep thought, or no thought at all. At the dinner table one night she asked him several questions about his various classes. All seemed well there. Finally she asked, "Jody is anything wrong? You are too quiet. What's going on?" He looked at her, got up, shook his head, and went to his room. The next afternoon Maria was watching for him to get home, she met him at the front doorsteps."I just baked a good peach pie for you." With her arms around him, they headed for the kitchen. "Did you have a nice day?" she asked. With his mouth full of pie and milk, he pointed his finger at her to wait. He began to tell her about his girl friend, Allison. Maria was so relieved. So this had been his problem, she thought.

After a few days, Jody got permission from his Mom to invite Allison for dinner one night. He had mentioned her several times in the past week. They had some classes together. He had also talked to Allison about his family. So on her arrival, everyone felt relaxed, and at ease. Jody placed his arm around her and made the introductions."Everyone, this is Allison, a friend I've told you about." He took a bow. "This is my mother, Maria. This is my grandmother Jo, and this is my grandfather, Paps. Most people call him Doc, but he's Paps to me. They had a great meal together, and talked freely about the zoo, the park, flowers and streams. Before Allison left, she asked Maria, "What should I call you?" Maria smiled."You can call me Maria, if you wish." Jody butt in, "Or you can call her Mom, if you wish." He turned to his mother and told her, "Allison, unlike me, has a Dad, but doesn't have a mother."

Later during the week, Jody asked his Mom if Allison's Dad could go with them on their planned day out. She said, "Of course. I like the girl. She seems a very nice person with great manners. Sure, you can invite her Dad. Then there will be six of us." She put her arms around her son and held him close. "You are so special to me. You know that, don't you?" "I have always known that." He replied. Maria's eyes filled with tears. She wiped her face, gave Jody a kiss on his cheek, and went to her room. She fell onto her knees by the bed and prayed."Thank You God for staying with me as I raised my son. He is a good person, and he knows right from wrong. Thank you that he has always been obedient and respectful. He is a caring person, and is never unkind or disrespectful to anyone. Thank You." She heard a noise in the kitchen. It was Jody making each of them a cup of cocoa. Together they sat down and sipped.

The six of them went in Jody's truck to the State Park. Jo carried a box of fried chicken and potato salad. Maria took a box of sandwiches. They also took a gallon of tea. Allison carried paper goods, and her Dad took ice.

Raymond Barfield was a tall, handsome man with blue eyes and dark curly hair. He assisted Maria in getting the picnic tables covered and placing the food upon them. Jo put ice in all the glasses, while Allison placed the paper plates and plastic forks. Everyone talked and laughed. Maria couldn't keep her eyes off Raymond. And every time she glanced at him, he was glancing at her. The six of them planned to go to church together the following Sunday. Jody and Allison cleaned off the table and put everything in order to leave for the zoo.

It was a long walk, but a great one. While everyone else was awed by the animals, Jo couldn't get her eyes off the trees, shrubbery, and flowers. She was also fascinated by the bubbling streams. It all brought back memories of her old home. She walked around another circle and then sat down on a bench beneath some tall trees with monkeys in the top of them. Allison said, "I'll sit with you Granny." Jody and Paps went one way; Maria and Raymond went another. Allison asked, "What was it like living on a farm? Jody said you always lived on a farm." Jo thought for a moment and then began.

"I was raised, for the most part, on a beautiful 300-acre farm. Pastures, fields, orchards, and streams made up the landscape; and for back ground was a wide variety of majestic trees surrounded by a pine forest. Situated about halfway between two creeks and a branch with a sandy bottom meandered through the farm. Though we called it Sandy Creek, I don't think that was official, and might not have been legal.

I try not to remember the work: plowing the fields, planting seed, hoeing the garden, gathering corn, shaking the peanuts, harrowing the pastures and orchards. There were however, a few fun things. Picking berries, fruits, vegetables, pecans, and the endless canning, were my favorites. Sawing logs, chopping, splitting, stacking wood were continuous chores. Carrying water from a spring to the house was daily routine. Rounding up cows every evening was not really work, depending on ones attitude. I did it because my sister was afraid of horses, cows, and anything else that moved. So I traded my dishwashing and ironing to her, and I went after the cows.

Once out of my Daddy's sight, I made those horses do tricks that would have scared the life out of him. He never did know what a trainer I was. Those four horses could stand on their hind legs, point their noses to the sky, and walk backwards and sideways. They could jump up and down, leap, and gallop with the wind. One of them could toss me right over her head. I could tie her to a post, beat the fire out of her, get back into the saddle, and run her until she was white with lather. Exhausted, her spirits calmed. The cattle would get so excited; they desired nothing more than to head for the pens. I loved horses, and fondly recall roundups.

A time I try to remember is spring. The doors and windows were swung open, and the house, from ceiling to floor, was scrubbed and cleaned. On Saturdays Mama took her five siblings to the woods, and gathered flowers. Along the banks of Sandy Creek violets grew in purple splendor. Blooming Dogwoods painted a white-wash throughout the woods and created endless vision. The beauty and fragrance of wild honeysuckle offered contentment to their guest. The woods, as a whole, served generous helpings of peace and tranquility. I never wanted to leave. Mama didn't either. We had to.

Back home glasses of violets adorned every table: fruit jars filled with spring water were hidden with the profusely blooming honeysuckle. Syrup cans held blossom-laden branches of dogwood. Our home became colorful and sweet. As the bouquets aged, their aroma became more pungent and floated through our rooms one Saturday to the next.

And then came winter casting her blanket over everything beautiful and blooming, snatching life from violets, dogwood, honeysuckle, and everything that blooms. But Spring returns and all of God's creation blooms again." Allison put her arms around Jo and said, "I love you Granny."

Chapter 2

Jo felt it was nap time and was ready to go home. The other four soon came to them. Paps asked "Is every body ready to go home?" Everyone said "A men!" Maria insisted that Raymond and Allison stay for a while. "Do you have any ice cream?" Allison wanted to know. Maria smiled."No, but you and Jody can go get some. And don't eat it all before you get back. I want some too." Maria was about to give Jody some money, but Raymond beat her to it, "I want some too." He sneered. After Jo and Paps, had gone home for a nap, the other four sat on the front porch and ate ice cream.

Raymond asked Maria if she would like to go to a movie. She said she would love it. Allison said, "I'd like to go to." Then Jody added, "I'd like to go too." Raymond laughed. You can both go if you want to, but not with Maria and me." A strange laugh rumbled through the porch before Jody said, "Sounds good to me. Allison, you can go with me." Off they went. "We will all meet back here." Raymond announced.

Jo and Paps woke up, and began to make plans. Jo called Maria to tell her that everyone would eat dinner at her house. She already had it planned and was presently in the kitchen. That sounded good to Maria who was too tired to worry about fixing a meal. After they got home from the movie, she and Raymond just laid back on the front porch in the rocking chairs. Raymond reached over and squeezed her hand."Wake up sweetheart, the phone is ringing." After dinner, Allison and Jody cleaned the kitchen. Raymond and Maria went back to her house. Raymond said to Allison, "Don't tarry too long, It's about time for us to go home," Jo asked Jody if he would make a cup of cocoa for the four of them. He did. As they sat at the table, Allison asked, "Granny will you tell me about chickens? I have never seen a chicken." Jo responded."Well darling you have missed a lot. I have wondered where are the chickens."

"What happened to the beautiful chickens that used to scratch in every yard? I loved them, and I miss them. It was from chickens that I learned the facts of life. From them I learned about people and their interactions, love, hate, humility and pride, work and play. I studied them through many hours of observation, just sitting on a door step watching without anything better to do.

There were in my Mother's yard, different breeds of chickens. Most however were mixed breeds varying in color and in size. The Plymouth Rocks were good egg producers and were a good meat breed. One of them adorned the dinner table every Sunday. The Rhode Island Reds were good winter layers and were used for cross-breading. We had White Leghorns and Black Leghorns and Brown Leghorns that were abundant layers. My Mother, without hesitation, would put a dozen eggs into a pound cake that weighed far more than a pound. For a family of seven, she cooked more than a dozen eggs every morning for breakfast, and then boiled as many for school lunches. Chickens, regardless to pedigree, were a very important contribution to my survival, as to my education.

Though the chickens were fed grain regularly, they did not depend on it. They still scratched contently and constantly over an acre of ground. They would come together for the free handouts, yet they were willing workers. The mother hens would teach their chicks to scratch for food by calling them with a cluck to witness the editable she uncovered. Very young I learned that I would be expected to scratch for a living. Handouts, if there were any, would not be enough. I would have to be a willing worker.

There is much love displayed by the mother hen. Not only does she work diligently to feed her chicks, she also stands ready to defend them. She will bravely attack snakes, cats or dogs that become a threat to her family. There may be a hundred chicks following six hens, but each one knows its mother, and each mother knows her chicks. Woe unto the chick that wanders from his brood and follows the wrong family. Mother hens will not tolerate a run-a-way chick.

The only hatred in the chicken yard is demonstrated among the roosters. The cocks are loaded with pride and valor. They strut around the hens showing off their gallantry. They love to crow in high places. They love to chase hens. They love to violate another rooster's territory, and they love to show heroic course in a fight. Yet, in a courtly manner, they are polite and attentive to young pullets.

We never had a rooster to lay an egg, but we did have some crowing hens. The crowing hens ended in a stewing pot. Young roosters ended in a frying pan. It was not wise to have too many cocks strutting among hens. Maybe it's true that a whistling woman and a crowing hen never come to a good end.

The poultry industry with it's commercial hatcheries, cold storage warehouses, and shipping methods have robbed the chicken yards, and I never see al live chicken anymore. Perhaps that is because I don't live in the country anymore. Many of our youngsters will never know the beauty or the education that can be seen and learned from the common fowl. A dead, naked chicken shows no beauty, no emotions, and no insights to life."

After Jo had finished, Jody looked at Allison."It's time for us to go." After they had left Jody said. "If you want to know, ask Jo." Allison laughed. Grabbed Jody by the arm and said, "I love to hear Granny talk. She is very smart. Paps was smiling. He loves to hear her talk too." Jody laughed and home they went. Raymond met them at his truck."It's about time you two showed up." Jody stood in the driveway until they drove off. As he entered the house, Maria called him. They needed a chat.

Do you know that Raymond has a lake house, boat shed, and a large boat?" He leered at her."Yes, I knew." She leered back, "Why didn't you tell me?" They both laughed, "Because I didn't know it would matter to you." Raymond had also asked Maria to go to the cabin with him." She told Jody."Did he want me and Allison to go along?" Marie looked at him, but said nothing. Jody jumped up and down. "O, my God, I think you just revealed something I've been thinking. You two have sort of fell for each other. Haven't you?" Maria shook her head and said "No, I have not fell for him, but I do like him. He's a very nice person, friendly, and respectful. We are friends, and that's it."Jody smiled at her and said."I don't think so. I think you should go camping with him. He needs a friend too." Maria glared at him. "To be in a three bedroom cabin is not camping." Jody pinched her ear and laughed. "Whatever you say Mom, but I think you should go. It would be a treat for you too." Maria hit him on the shoulder. "Alright, I will."

The next day Raymond dropped by the hospital where Maria worked, as a nurse, and took her to lunch. He asked her to set a date for their lake-side trip. She laid her hand over his, and said," I'm off on Friday." Raymond squeezed her hand and said."Friday it is." Any day would be good for Raymond, since he owned and operated Barfield Electric Company, he could take any day off he choose, or as many days. "Can we stay until Sunday?" Maria replied, "No. I'm sorry, but one day at a time." He bumped knees with her from under the table. "As you say, Madam." As he dropped Maria off at the hospital, she asked, "Dinner tonight?" Raymond smiled."Yes, where, and when?" "At my house around six o'clock." She replied. He walked her to the entrance door, kissed the top of her head, and left.

Maria called her parents to come for dinner. She called Raymond and asked him to bring Allison. In the kitchen, she was cooking, singing, smiling, and even dancing around, as Jody entered. She was usually in the kitchen when he got home. She loved living near the college. Her son could come home every night. Now and then he'd come home late if he and Allison went someplace together. He was never too late because of home work to be done. He was making good grades. His Mom and Grandparents were so proud of him.

The door bell rang and Jody ran to open the door. Allison had picked up a pound cake and went on into the kitchen with it. She sniffed, "Something smells good." Jody sneaked up behind her and, grabbed her arm and said, "It's me." Maria pleaded, "Will you two get out of here? Raymond can help me finish the cooking." On their way out, Allison proclaimed, "My Dad is a good cook." Raymond took Maria into his arms and kissed her on the cheek. "What can I do?" He asked. At that time Jo and Paps came into the kitchen. "Smells good in here Jo said." Maria turned to Raymond, "It must not have been Jody after all."

The six had a great meal together. As they were about to finish, Jody asked his Mom," Have you decided what day you're going camping?" Maria snapped at him. "We are not going camping, I told you." She looked at her Mom. "Raymond and I are going to his lake house Friday." "You're not going to spend the night?" Jody inquired. Maria shook her finger at him, but said nothing. Paps added to the conversation. "That will be a good break for both of you. And you both need a break from you know who." Everybody laughed. Jody said to Allison, "That wouldn't mean you and me of course."Jo looked at him. "Then who? Surely not me." Jody peeked at her, and said, "I think so." Jo reached over and tapped the top of his head with a spoon. Jody said, "You better watch out. After next week I'll no longer be a teenager or a kid. I'll be a man, and will stand my ground. Right Paps?" Everyone laughed, and Paps replied, "In my book, you are already a man, and a very good on" After that every one began to leave the table. Jo and Paps cleaned up the mess.

Out on the boat, Maria was fascinated by the bubbling streams, fish flouncing around, the breeze that tossed her hair all over her head, and Raymond smiling at her. "Is my hair pretty?" She asked Raymond. He replied," You are always beautiful, even when your hair is standing straight up." They sailed all over the lake. Maria felt comfortable standing on the dock with Raymond's arms around her. They fixed a snack for lunch and went out on the dock to eat it. Raymond cooked out on the dock that evening. They sat in a swing and talked, looking around at the majestic views that surrounded them. Maria noticed a large strange bus parked under a shelter. She asked about it. "That's my camper." Raymond said. Maria decided then, that Jody already knew about it. That's why he kept mentioning camping. "I want to see it," She said. She was curious, why would one want a cabin and a camper. She was awed as they went through the camper. She had never seen one. What surprised her most was the kitchen and the bathroom. Something inside of her would not calm down. She had to go camping in a real camper. Back on the dock, she began asking questions about camping. Raymond had a little butterfly stirring up his emotions.

"Camping is a lot of fun. It gives one a chance to see the whole country. The different landscapes offer a variety of great views." Now, Maria's emotions were really churning. Raymond sprung forth, "The second or third week in October is an ideal time to go camping in the Appalachian Mountains that extend across North Carolina. The Black Mountains, one of the only two distinct peaks left in the Appalachians, hold Mount Mitchell, the loftiest peak. The air is refreshingly cool; the woods are a sight to behold and the meandering streams flowing over and around beds of rock offer a serenity not easily found.

Camping is the escape, that getting away; from the humdrum of routine that entraps most of us. It's a freedom that promotes a profound and effective meditation that not only includes self soul-searching, but also a deeper awareness of the great Creator and a closer relationship with Him.

Man may attempt to paint the mountains and hillsides and rocks and trees, but his work will not be comparable to the true Artist. Canvas, though it may reflect beauty and cause moods, it cannot offer the environment, the purity, the absolute beauty and awesome sensations that the woods themselves can do. Man, at his best, is a little better than nothing if he compares his work with the true and realistic work by the Creator of all work. But pleasure is attained from dabblers who try to capture a part of the great world onto a bit of canvas. Being a dabbler myself, and intercourse with nature proves to me how limited man is. The joys of camping, however, is in no way trying to compete with the Master, but to enjoy His greatness by being surrounded by and blended into His creation.

Eating bacon and eggs under a brilliant and majestic maple tree is a treat that we all deserve. Boiling coffee in an old pot along river banks is so delightful. It should be an obligation to every human being. I wish that every family in the whole world would take a few days a year and go camping to discover a rest and a peace that surpasses all naps.

Surrounding ourselves with that which God made, and getting away from that which man made are experiences we can cling to. The beauty and the sensation will come back to us at any time in the future that we recall them. Buildings and pavements, telephones and televisions, exhaust fumes and smoke stacks, and other man-made things do not offer pleasing memories from which to muse.

Unique exposures are found on camping trips as we interact with nature. Memories are deeply ingrained within us. They never fade away as long as thought is present. Seeing vari-colored flowers, leaves, tree trunks, rocks, and weeds paints lasting beauty. And when these things reflect in water, they paint waterfalls and streams that are too awesome to ever forget.

Our relationship with nature does not have to be on the mountain. It does not have to be October. The wonders of nature are varied forms, locations, and seasons. To see a sunrise or a sunset at the ocean offers a beauty and peace that often makes me cry a little."

Maria thought about the paintings that she had noticed on Raymond's walls. So he is the dabbler. All of the paintings were outdoor scenes. She wondered if he and his wife did much traveling. He had told her that his wife had died of cancer when Allison was six years old. He never said anything else about her, and Maria didn't ask. "Would you like to go on a camping trip to the Grand Canyon, Yellow Stone, Painted Dessert, and Petrified Forest? Carlsbad Caverns or Niagara Falls?" Maria screamed, "All of them. I've never done any traveling except to college and back." Raymond asked," When would you like to go?" She thought for a minute, then suggested, "In the summer, I suppose, when the kids will be free to go with us. That's not exactly what Raymond had in mind. He gave her a mean look. She got the message. "We'll make plans later, but I do want to go. And I will pay half of the expenses." Raymond gave her another mean look.

Chapter 3

"Mom, would anyone care if Allison went to church with us Sunday?" Jody wanted to know. "Of course not, we would all be happy to have her go." When Sunday came, Maria asked Jody if he was picking up Allison."No." he answered "Her Dad will drop her off." Raymond came in with Allison."May I go too? I'd like to be included." Maria had wanted him and Allison to attend church with them. She placed her arm around him, and said, "Of course, you can. In fact, I want you to go with us, and sit with me." He kissed Maria's nose. They heard some snickering, and looked around. There stood the kids watching them. Maria stomped her foot at Jody. Laughing, she said, "Get out of here." On their way out, Jody started singing. "Did you see what I saw?" That was funny to Raymond, and he grabbed Maria into his arms and gave her a most appropriate kiss. Then the two headed for the church.

Pastor Harris preached a fantastic sermon—as usual. The choir was excellent. Pastor Harris noticed the visitors and was awed at the attention they gave him. He spoke of a revival that should be scheduled. "Everyone needs a revival." He screamed. Raymond took the six out to dinner, and invited the Pastor and his great wife, Tonya, to go with them. They graciously accepted. Jo and Paps invited them to their house for desert. She had baked a peach pie and plenty of it. As soon as they had finished eating, Raymond asked Pastor Harris exactly what a revival meant. He had never been to one. The pastor said, "Sure Raymond, I'd be happy to explain that to you.

"At least once a year everybody needs a revival. That's not to say we don't need to be revived more often, for the need is constant; but once a year it is a necessity. It is the necessity that makes me cry, for I need a revival too; for this I feel sorrowful. If revivals were only to stir up faith among the faithless, I would feel more joyful; but knowing that the revival's purpose is for more preaching disturbs me. Though revival means to come, it also means to bring back.

Our world is filled with hiding places, and too often we seek them. Often too, we aimlessly wander into them. Therefore, we need to be brought back into the light of awareness. Our consciousness, after a decline of healthy thought, need to be renewed. So a revival is needed to jolt our minds, to remind us of who we are, to turn us around, and to give us a push. Because we veer from the straight path onto the winding one, or we linger too long at a crossroad, we have to be alerted that we may return to the flourishing life that exhibits effective leading, teaching, interacting, and caring.

Why we wander is an ageless question, one that goes back to the creation of man. It is not that we are ignorant. We have had great leaders and teachers who have, not only set perfect examples before us, but who have also told us in understandable and believable messages the right life to live, the right road to travel, and the only destination truly worthy of our efforts. Yet, because we are human beings endowed with freedom of thought, we wander.

In our worldly affiliations, we are less disobedient. If our bosses hand us a list of guidelines and speak of other expectations, we read, we listen, we believe, we learn, we obey; not to do so would cost us our jobs. We are coherent to our work schedules; we attend meetings as an extra measure of our security. We are dependable and we are loyal. We strive to please the boss lest his favors should be sprinkled thinly. Vigorously, we strive to a little more than what is expected, for we do not want to be left on the bottom rung of the echelon ladder. To clime near the top is ideal; the awards there are more desirable.

If we were so enthusiastic and dedicated to our Christian life, our rewards would be countless. They would be more pure, more sure, and would be everlasting. Jesus Christ handed us a list of guideline, He gave us simple instructions, and He promised the most desirable rewards. We can become His heirs and inherit His kingdom. Earthly bosses cannot make such promises. Yet, we display more loyalty, respect, and honors to Mr. Boss than we do for the Master.

Mr. Boss will surely fire us if we are not obedient; and for the same reason, the Master will use His fire. In spite of these facts, however, it seems that we are more concerned about losing our jobs than losing our souls. I wonder why."

Jody thought the pastor would never finish, and when he did, the kids got up and left. The Harris's soon left. Since it was past time for her parents nap, Marcia and Raymond left. Raymond began asking a few questions Christianity. They talked for a couple of hours. He was most impressed by the message from Pastor Harris. The next Sunday, the two Barfield's accepted Christ and became members of the church. Both were baptized, and went home a new person.

Summer came and lives began to change. Paps and Jo shared their plans. They were going to New Orleans to visit Jo's niece, Marcia, and her family. They would be gone several days, because there was much to do and see. Jo asked Jody if he would like to go with them. He didn't appear too interested. Paps began telling him about the area. He told him about the French Quarters, the canal, the Dixie Land Jazz that played on Basin, Bourbon, and Ramparts streets. That didn't appear to strengthen Jody's interest. Jo and Maria got together and Jo told her, "I'm sorry, but we can't talk Jody into going with us." Maria mused for a moment, "I was so sure he would want to go."

That night Jody walked into the kitchen where Maria was mixing up something for them to eat. "I thought it was about time for you. You look like something is wrong." Jody kept quiet until they sat down to eat. "Mom, Granny and Paps want me to go with them to New Orleans, and I want to know what your plans are while they are gone." He laughed at Maria. "They are not the only ones who want me to go, you do too. So what's going on? I'm not a five year old, you know." That was funny to Maria. "That's right, you are not a kid any more, but you are not quiet twenty either. She started eating and thinking. "Mom, you didn't answer my question." Jody remarked. Maria looked at him, "I really don't know. Raymond and I have talked about a few things, but no decisions have been made. We might just wait until Mom and Dad get back. Someone needs to keep an eye on things."

Sitting in the back yard swing, Raymond asked Maria, "Is Jody going with his Grandparents?" "No." she snapped. "He doesn't want to go." Raymond laid his hand on her shoulder. "Why don't we plan our trip and take the kids with us? This could be the last time they'd want to follow us. It could be our last time to have a great get-together with them. They both know that we are up to something, and they want to be a part of it. We may look back some day and realize it's the best thing we ever did." Maria put both arms around him, and said, "Let's do it." Raymond glared at her, "I don't even know what our plan is. Do you?" They both laughed.

Jo and Paps took off early Monday morning. The other four left early the following Monday morning. They couldn't make comfortable sleeping arrangements in the camper for four, so they left in Raymond's two-seated truck. The back of the truck had a cover over it, and offered sufficient space for luggage. Jody and Allison were most excited to be going to the Grand Canyon. They had already done their research, and knew what to expect. They stayed over night at hotels along the way with Maria and Jody sharing one room, Raymond and Allison sharing another.

Their first stop was Petrified Forest National Park along the Little Colorado River. "The forest contains six separate areas of petrified coniferous tree trunks lying on the ground." Jody began explaining. Raymond was listening to him. And Jody continued. "Some of the tree trunks are six feet in diameter, and are one hundred feet long. One such trunk forms a bridge, the Agate Bridge." Allison put in her comment. "It's amazing to see so many trees, limbs, and chips that have turned into stone." Raymond patted Allison on her head, and said, "I'm sure glad you two came along."

The Grand Canyon was the next stop. Allison began explaining to her Dad that the Grand Canyon was an enormous valley in Arizona excavated by the Colorado River. "The canyon is approximately two hundred, and seventeen miles long, four to eighteen miles wide, and more than a mile deep." After catching her breath, she continued to explain that the entire canyon was impressively beautiful, containing towering buttes, mesas, and valleys within its main gorge. The canyon cuts deeply through an arid plateau which lies between five thousand and nine thousand feet above sea level. Colorado River flows through the lowest portions of the canyon. The canyon was caused by erosion of the river. Nine separate rock areas can be seen. The extreme variation of color is awesome. In the park one can find deer, antelope, cougar, and mountain sheep.

"We've about seen Arizona." Maria advised. "Yes, but not too far into New Mexico is Carlsbad Caverns." Allison advised. Raymond didn't appear to hear her. "I was thinking about turning around and heading back home. It's been a long drive, and a week away from home is long enough." He turned to Maria."What do you think?" Before Maria could speak, Jody butted in."I'd like to see the caverns. Several million bats inhabit the caverns and emerge nightly. The caverns area consists of nearly forty seven hundred acres. It's a National Park and the largest known subterranean labyrinth in the world. There are more than thirty seven miles of connecting corridors and chambers that have been explored." Raymond glanced at him. "Smart boy. You really did your home work, didn't you?" Allison responded."So did I. The deepest level is over a thousand feet below the surface of the earth. The Big room is about four thousand feet long and more than six hundred feet wide, and reaches a height of two hundred, and eighty five feet containing a variety of stalactites and stalagmites. The most notable is the Crystal Spring Dome, and Rock of Ages which has several levels and rooms." Raymond was speeches. "O.K. The caverns it is." Maria placed her arm around Raymond and whispered. "Aren't you glad we brought the kids?" He drew her closer to him, and whispered back. "Not particular." They both laughed and followed the kids.

"Jody, you do the driving. Give me a break. You're Mom and I will sit in the back seat for a change." Jody bumped shoulders with Raymond and snickered. "What if Allison and I don't want to sit in the front seat?" Raymond pulled Maria a little closer, and answered. "It doesn't matter what you want. I'm having it my way for a change. Jody grabbed Allison's hand. "Listen to him. I bet it's been his way as far back as you can remember. Believe me; I've lived in the same territory." She replied, yep." Raymond reached over and pulled her hair. Maria responded."I don't recall you ever living that life. I thought it was me." Raymond announced," Everyone in the truck. Lookout bats, here we come."

As soon as all was settled, Maria laid her head on Raymond's shoulder and fell asleep. Jody saw his Mom from the rear view mirror. "Look." He said to Allison."Just what I figured. In less than two minutes your Dad will be asleep too. When we get ready to eat or take a pit stop, I'll jam on the brakes and pitch both of them onto the floor." "Make sure they fall on the floor, and not on me," Allison remarked. Raymond reached over and pulled Jody's ear. "If you don't be careful, I'll put both of you out, and I'll take over." Jody was amused. He said, "You want be awake long enough to take over." Things got quiet. Jody looked behind him. Raymond was asleep.

The caverns were more massive than they had imagined, even though they had been given abundant information before arriving. The four walked into ever trail and explored ever level. They stayed late to see the bats soar from the caves. They had to return early the next morning so Jody could make sure the bats returned. "Do you want to go to New Orleans from here?" Maria wanted to know. "No, no, no" Raymond replied. "I am ready for home." Jody handed Raymond the truck keys. "It's your time to drive, Dad." Maria felt a little uncomfortable to hear that. Raymond gave a broad smile."O.K. son, I'll take the keys." Jody and Allison got into the back seat and talked about the caverns and bats for the rest of the day.

Chapter 4

Jo and Paps were already home when the other four arrived. Jody drove on down to his grandparents. The women went to the kitchen, the men relaxed on the porch. Endless conversations flowed throughout the house. Jo and Paps had a great trip. Seeing Marcia and her family meant much to them. Jo greatly appreciated the graciousness of the children. Never had she known a more respectful, considerate, and loving family.

"How did your trip turn out?" Jo asked. Maria was tired; she gave a short reply, "We all had a great time." Allison looked at her. "Is that all?" Maria yawned. "It's all for now. I'm tired."As soon as they had eaten, they all went home and went to bed.

Before Raymond left, he told Maria that he would pick her up, and take her out to dinner. Maria told Jody and asked him to take Allison out. He told her those arrangements were already taken care of. To bed she went. She asked Jody to wake her up by four o'clock. He laughed. "Sorry Mom, but I want be here. Allison and I are going to the movie. Raymond knocked on her door at five o'clock and startled her. She jumped out of bed, grabbed her robe, and ran to the door. "What took you so long?" He asked, and then added, "You sure look cute in that pink floral robe." He stepped inside. Maria closed the door, and then noticed that her robe was open. She had not tied it well. She glanced at herself and saw that she only had on her panties and a tee shirt. She ran to her room, while Raymond almost lost his breath trying to smoother a big laugh. When she came back into the living room, Raymond commented, "You look beautiful, but no more than you did when I first walked in." He got up off the couch and took her into his arms. "You don't need to be embarrassed, I'm no stranger. I'm your best friend, and I love you very much. So, if I happen to catch you half dressed, don't worry about it. No one will ever know it but you and me".

He released her, and she asked, "Why do you love me?" Without any hesitation, he replied. "Because of what I just saw. I already knew you were beautiful outside all your clothing, but to discover that beauty flowing all over your body really ran my blood pressure up." Maria attempted to leave the room, but Raymond went after her. "I'm Hungry, let's go."

At the restaurant, Maria was a bit too quiet. Raymond talked about their trip. "Maria, you'll never know how glad I am that the four of us went on that trip together. At first, I really didn't want the kids to go, but now, I thank God that they did. It was the best trip I ever had." He got Maria's attention when he thanked God. "I agree with you, I feel the same. They made the trip much more fun than it would have been without them. One thing for sure, they kept us laughing." Raymond silently thanked God again that Maria had settled down. Their dinner was served. Maria looked at her plate. What did she order? Raymond had a T-bone steak. She looked again at her own plate, and then asked Raymond "What did I order?" He looked at her plate and said, "I don't know, but it looks like a broiled bat."

Jo and Paps sat on their front porch and talked about their trip. They talked mostly about Maria's trip. Jo asked Paps, Do you think Maria and Raymond will get married?" Paps responded, "I am almost sure of it." Jo added, "I really hope they do. Maria has been single long enough. Believe me; I know the loneliness of spending twenty years alone." Paps was silent for a few minutes, then asked, "Isn't she about twice twenty?" Jo snapped, "Yes. You know what I mean. Jody will be twenty next Friday, and Maria is thirty nine." Paps added, "She sure did a great job of teaching Jody through his twenty years. He is a very good person. I am so proud of the person he became. And the credit goes to Maria." Jo went to the kitchen and returned with each of them a glass of iced tea. As Paps sipped his tea, he asked, "What do you think about Jody and Allison? Will they get married?" Jo laughed," I've thought about that too. It looks that way right now, but anything can happen by the time they get out of college." Paps thought for a moment, and then proclaimed, "My guess is that they will split soon." Jo looked up and said "We'd better hush, here they are."

Jody and Allison come upon the porch."Would you like some iced tea?" Jo asked. They both said, "Yes." Jo went back to the kitchen, then back again with the tea.

What have you two been up to?" She inquired. "We just got back from seeing a movie. Before that, we went out to eat." Allison responded. Where did you eat?" Paps asked. "Paps," Jody began, "Did you and granny ever eat at Jack's barbeque?" "No. I don't think so." Paps answered. "You have to go there. It's really good food, and the service is good too." He explained to Paps just the right way to get there. Jo cut him short. "Where are your parents?" They both shook their head. "The last I heard, they were going out for dinner too. I don't know where they are. Again, they didn't ask for my permission." Jody explained. Paps smiled."There will be other days like that."

"Granny, are you ever going to plant another garden?" Jody wanted to know. She responded. "Paps and I have talked about it. There might be enough space in the back yard for planting a few vegetables. We're going to look into it. We will have to get a garden tiller first." Jody asked, "Will you plant some squash?" He then turned to Allison. "Have you ever eaten squash?" She said, "Yes, my granny used to cook it. Sometimes she would fry it. I love it fried." "Me too." Jody shouted. Jo was amazed at those two. "Let me tell you about the squash." She began.

"Never have I been more excited about any one thing than I am about the squash. Until last October, I had never given any thoughts whatsoever to squashes. I merely cooked those yellow crook-necks with onions, ate them, and forgot them. A trip to the mountains changed my attitude. To me, the extreme shades of red, yellow and orange that splashes across countryside is more spectacular than the Grand Canyon. I have seen that too. Last fall, however, I became aware of these same splendid colors in squashes. They were displayed in numerous pyramids along the highways, mountain tops, and in valleys. I bought some of those beauties and brought them home to use for decorations. I would not have cooked them, had I known how. Later, being somewhat advanced with necessary obligations, I tackled the squash to expend my sphere of knowledge and to utilize leisure time. I should not have. I loathe wasted time, but more than that, I loathe confusion. And that's what the squash is. With one bit of information giving birth to another, I soon found myself within a maze that had no exit.

The name" squash" is of American Indian origin. The squash has been developed in many varieties and yields fruits of widely differing forms and sizes. The summer squash has a soft rind and includes the yellow crookneck, white or yellow scallop, and the white or green button. It's the winter varieties that offer such an array of color and shape. The Hubbard, Boston marrow, Turban, Butternut, and Crown are among the most beautiful. The Turban and the Crown are of brilliant reds, yellows and greens. These may be used to enhance any holiday décor, but are exceptionally awesome when used in center pieces. They keep well and can be cooked later in several tasty dishes. To learn that the squash, the cucumber, and the watermelon are, if not sisters, cousins, confused me. They are all members of the gourd family, as well as the pumpkin and the muskmelon. The squash is a gourd? That's right!"

Allison was fascinated, as she always was with Jo's conversations. Jody was not so impressed, and after a few minutes of catching his breath, he said to Allison, "It's about time we hit the road. We'll go by my house first to see if they are there. If they are not, then we'll go to your house." They both hugged Jo and Paps, and then left.

Maria and Raymond were at her house when the kids arrived. They had been discussing plans for Jody's birthday. To have a picnic at the lake was Raymond's choice. To go on a day and night camping trip was Maria's choice. She would sleep on the bed with Allison, Raymond could sleep on the couch, and Jody would sleep on the floor. She would take some quilts and extra pillows for him to lie on. Raymond pushed his idea. "But at the lake three of you could sleep on a bed, and I would sleep on the couch. That way no one would have to sleep on the floor." Maria threw a magazine at him, and said, "Hush!" "What are you two arguing about?" Jody inquired. Raymond responded. "We are having a fist fight over what we'll do for your birthday." Jody laughed. "Why didn't someone ask me? Let's take a short trip in the camper." Raymond threw the magazine at him. Allison said, "Let's all go to the lake for an overnight trip." Raymond threw both hands up."What ever! What ever!" He walked over to the window and stared outside. A beautiful day out there, but a stormy one inside. He turned around and commanded, "Jody, since it's your birthday, you call the shot." Jody took a bow and said, "To the Grand Ole Opera in Nashville we'll go." Everyone fell to the floor!

Maria got with her parents and told them about the mix up. They were both very concerned. Jo said, "Well, if any of your choices are met, that would put his grand parents totally out of the picture. We are his family too, and we certainly love him. He is our only grand child." Paps promoted Jo's comment. He looked at Jo and said, "I support your comment. Jody belongs to us too." Now, Maria didn't know which way to turn, but she knew better than to throw anything at her Mom. Paps said he needed to talk with Jody. He could bring a closure to the Grand Ole Opera idea.

After Maria left, Paps called Jody and asked him to drop by alone. Jody was ebullient, for he knew what Paps wanted. He also knew that his Mom had just left there. More than that, he knew that Paps could solve the problem. Paps remarked."I hear you would like to go to the Grand Ole Opera for your birthday. That surprises me. I never knew that you were interested in Country Music." Jody laughed."Paps, that is the least of my interest, but it did put and end to an ongoing controversy. That was my aim." Paps gave Jody a big hug and said."Well, you rang your goal." As Jody was about to leave, Paps added," Don't make your final decision until you consider the Kentucky Derby. If that turns out to be your decision, the trip is on me. And please let the rest of the family know that your grand parents are going too." Jody was so excited; he grabbed Paps and gave him a big squeeze. Jo yelled, "Turn him loose. He's having trouble breathing. They all laughed and Jody then grabbed Jo and held her close. "I love you both," he said as he went out the door.

When Jody got home, Raymond was still there. Jody knew that they had been trying to sooth their differences. He sat down at the table with them where they were sipping on hot coffee. Maria knew where he had been. After all, she was the one who set it up. "Would you like something to drink?" she asked. "Not really." He muttered. After a moment of silence, he said "Mom, Paps and Granny are planning to take me to the Kentucky Derby for my birthday. I think Paps really wants to go. He said he had always wanted to go, but never did. He wants to take me with him. I told him I would greatly appreciate that. He also said the rest of you can go, if you wish to. I think Granny will enjoy it more if you two and Allison go with us." Maria and Raymond were speechless. Finally, Raymond reached across the table and placed his hand over Maria's. "That sounds good to me. I, too, have always wanted to go to the Kentucky Derby, but never did," Maria almost went into tears. Finally, she was able to speak, and said, "Sounds good to me. I will go." Jody jumped up, danced all over the kitchen, and yelled, "Kentucky Derby it is." As he headed for his room, he announced," Paps will make all the arrangements. He will get the tickets. So let him know," Raymond promised "I'll get with him, and I'll get the tickets. Well, three anyway. Raymond went home a happy man.

Maria had to be at work early to replace an employee who was sick. She got Jody to drive her to the hospital.

She didn't like to drive before daylight nor after dark. Jody took her. He wanted to be at the college early, so it worked for both of them. Ahead of his regular schedule, Dr. Dawkins came in. He was surprised to see Maria already on duty. "Is there anything wrong?" He asked. "No, I came in early to fill in for Colleen who is sick." He looked at her with a warm penetrating smile. "Have you had breakfast?" Why would he care, she pondered. "No, I got up too early to eat." He patted her on the shoulder, and said, "Follow me." They went to the cafeteria and ate breakfast together. He was far more talkative than usual. She told him that her son had driven her to work. "Tell me about your son." This really amazed Maria. Why would Dr. Dawkins care to know anything about her son? She thought for a moment, and then briefly said that Jody was her only child, and was a medical student at Smithville. She cut it short as possible. At that moment, a very loud speaker announced that Dr. Dawkins was needed in the delivery room immediately. He got up and left. Maria was relieved.

As Raymond took Maria back to work after taking her to lunch, they were observed by Dr. Dawkins who also worked in the birthing center. He had seen the two of them together before and now wondered if anything serious bonded them. He had worked close with Maria, and liked her very much. She was dedicated to her job and did it well.

The blue and white uniform she wore looked good on her. And fit her fine. She was always on the move, and hadn't appeared to notice him except when they were working side by side. Knowing that she was not married, he began to ponder. He was not married either, but Maria never appeared to notice that. Perhaps she didn't know it. He would work on that. As Raymond was about to leave, he patted Maria on her shoulder. At that time, Dr. Dawkins walked up to them. "Did you two have a good lunch?" He inquired. Raymond gave him a strange look. "Yes, we did." He snapped.

Maria introduced the two, thanked Raymond, and walked off. So did Raymond. He turned his head toward her and said. "I'll pick you up at five." "Thank you." She responded. Then her brain began to spin. Why did Raymond remind her that he'd pick her up at five? She already knew that. It would be her only way home, since she didn't drive her own car that morning. Did he, for some reason, resent Dr. Dawkins, and if so, why. She and Dr. Dawkins worked together, and that's all. She did like and respected him because he was so correct in his decisions. Where there was doubt, and many situations were, he would come up with a well-working plan. Did Raymond resent Dr. Dawkins approaching them? Why?

She was alerted to the delivery room. Another miracle was about to happen. "We've got twins fighting to be the first one out." Dr. Dawkins told her. "Are there any complications?" She asked. He answered "Yes, but nothing that the two of us can't handle." His smile was a bit different, and for the first time, his arm touched hers. The delivery was successful. The music surrounded the hospital that everyone would know that two more infants had successfully entered the world. Dr. Dawkins said to Maria. "Let's go find a cup of coffee or a milk shake. We are both a bit tensed up. You did a marvelous job. I might not could have managed that without you." Maria was mesmerized. He had never asked her to have coffee with him, nor anything else. She went with him. The two of them had a great break together. She looked at her watch. Raymond would not be there for another half hour. She would have to be at the front desk by then.

Dr. Dawkins walked with her to the front desk, which was not unusual, but he was a bit too friendly. Raymond was waiting for her. "Are you ready?" He asked without noticing Dr. Dawkins. Dr. Dawkins patted Maria on the shoulder. "Thank you." he said, and then walked away. He had never before put his hand on her. She took Raymond's hand into hers. "Did you have a nice day?" He muttered."O.K." He parked in front of her house and sit waiting for her to get out of his truck."You're not getting out?" She asked. He shook his head and drove off.

Chapter 5

Jody was home alone. "Where is Raymond?" Maria replied, "He had some things to do." "Mom, did you know my summer break begins tomorrow. Today was my last day of classes until September?" Yes, she knew that, but hadn't given much thought to it. "I'll have to go to work now, then our trip to the Kentucky Derby, then back to work for Raymond." During the summer, Jody worked for Raymond. He was, by no means, an electrician, but he was good at doing odd jobs around the office. He learned well, and only had to be told once. He ran the errands, and soon knew his way around. He set up appointments and kept everything on schedule. "Why don't you become an electrician?" Raymond asked him. "I'm thinking about it, but don't tell Paps. If I don't become a doctor, he will have a heart attack." Raymond seriously asked, "What would your decision be?" Jody threw his arms up and told him. "I really don't know. There are two or three areas I've been thinking about. Please don't mention this to Mom." Raymond took Jody's hand, and said, "Trust me."

She sat there at the table for awhile thinking. Being a registered nurse, she had a good job that paid her well. Being the managing nurse of the birthing department, she enjoyed every day. She loved the lullaby tune that rang out all over the hospital as a baby was born. She had followed her mother's footsteps into the field of nursing, and she never regretted it. Now living so near to Smithville, made it so much easier for her son to attend college. She reflected back to her own experiences at Smithville. It was almost more than she could handle, but she did. Now, back there as a managing nurse made her feel that, in spite of all the hard times, she accomplished far more than she ever expected. She patted herself on the cheek and whispered, "Well done ole girl."

Paps and Jo drove to Maria's late in the evening. No one was there except the two of them. That is strange, Jo thought. At least one of the Barfield's is usually here. She was glad the four of them would be alone. Paps reminded them."Our trip to the Derby is two weeks away, but I haven't heard it mentioned since we first planned it. Is it still on?" Jody immediately replied. "Yes." Paps added."Well, let's talk about it. I have the six tickets. How are we going? Who's driving? Motel registrations have been made. So let's put it together. Maria asked if Raymond had talked with him about this lately. Paps said "No, but he did say they were going. Is anything wrong?" She was silent for a moment, and then said, "I don't know. He's not been around for several days. I've called him, but he doesn't return my calls." Jody added, "I have wondered if something was wrong. He's been acting strange at work lately. Mom, do you and Raymond have a problem?" Maria shook her head, and said "I don't know." Jo said, "We will need to know if they are going with us, since we already have the tickets." Jody responded. "Raymond said he'd pay for half the tickets, and I know he will."

After her parents left, Maria said to Jody, "Allison hasn't been around in quiet a while. Anything wrong there?" Before he could answer, the door bell rang. Jody ran to the door. Allison was there. She came in and said to Maria, "It's so good to see you. It's been a long time." She hugged Maria. "I was just asking about you." Maria said. "It's been a mass of confusion lately at the college. I am so happy to have a summer break, and time to think." Maria finally asked, "How is your Dad?" Allison said that he was not feeling well. He had a cold and a sore throat. "How long has he been sick?" Maria wanted to know. "Since yesterday." Allison said. As Allison was about to leave, Jody asked her about the trip. As far as she knew, she and her Dad were going with them.

Jody talked with his Mom about Allison. She was happy with her educational decision. She withdrew from the medical field to become a math teacher. Her mother had been a math teacher at the college

Allison was attending, and Allison decided to climb that ladder. Her Dad approved of the change. During the summer she worked at the local library. She loved to read and she loved children. Having lost her mother, and then her grandmother, Maria and Jo were very close to her. They always reached out to her, and included her in family activities. She felt a love that was long needed. Helping her to get into the church was her greatest experience. She never had so many friends until she became active in the church.

After Maria's chat with Jody, she got into her car and went to Raymond's. She rang the door bell four times before he came to the door. He was surprised to see her standing there. "What a surprise." He said. "Come on in. I'm very glad to see you." She smiled and replied, "It's good to see you. It's been too long. Allison said you had a sore throat. I brought you some lemon aid" He thanked her, took the jar from her, and carried it to the kitchen. He came back and asked Maria to sit down. "Not before you give me a hug. The lemon aid is not free, you know." Raymond took her into his arms, and with a trembling voice, said "I'm so glad you came." Maria kissed him on the cheek and remarked, "What would you do if someone you loved didn't, or wouldn't return your calls?" He held her closer, and with still a trembling voice responded."I'm so sorry. I didn't know what to do." Maria released herself, and sat down on the couch. She told him how surprised she was that a man of his intelligence didn't know what to do. She thought he knew how to use the phone, or drive to her house. She glared at him, and he sat down beside her. He laughed at her, and pulled her onto his lap. Maria knew he had a weak voice. She placed her cheek against his and assured him that she still loved him. She pulled herself to her feet, and left. At the door, she turned back toward Raymond and said, "Drop by if you ever want to. We'll be leaving Monday for the Derby. I want you to go, and I hope you will. Let me know." Raymond was speechless.

While Maria was eating her bacon and egg sandwich, the doorbell rang. She was too excited, knowing it was Raymond. She ran to the door. Dr. Dawkins stood there with a broad smile on his face, and a bouquet of roses. Maria was shocked. She placed the flowers on a table, thanked him, and asked him to be seated. How glad she was to be home alone. Jody wouldn't be home until late. She asked Dr. Dawkins if he would like something to drink. He replied that he would like a glass of wine. "What kind do you have?" He asked. "I'm sorry." Maria said," but your only choice here is coffee, tea, or lemon aid."He gave her a strange look, "Let's skip the drink for now." Maria responded, "That's fine," and sat down opposite to him in a chair. She kept wondering what he was doing there. "What are you doing this evening, just wandering around?" His reply was, "You got that right. It took a lot of rambling around to find your neighborhood, or your house. How long have you lived in this area?" She thought for a moment, and then said, "We've been here about two years. We moved here to be near the college my son attends." He looked over the living room with a smirk on his face, then asked, "Your son is planning to become a medical doctor? I hope he makes it. It's not easy, and takes a load of money. Your salary will not near cover it." Maria snapped back at him, "That is not a problem. It's already been taken care of.

They talked about the birthing center at the hospital. Then he asked if she would like to go out to dinner with him. She said she was sorry, but her son would soon be home and they would eat together at home, since that plan had already been established. Dr. Dawkins looked around, "I was surprised that you live in this area. I had thought that you surely would live in a more elite neighborhood, and a larger house, but I'm sure when you moved here, you didn't know the areas that well." Just as Maria was about to throw him out, the door bell rang. "Well," Maria said, "It's about time for you to go. And if you ever decide to come back, call me first." He got the message, got up and headed for the door. As Maria opened the door, there stood Raymond. When he saw Dr. Dawkins, he turned to leave. Maria grabbed his arm and held it tight. "Thanks for the roses."Maria said, as Dr. Dawkins was leaving.

She pulled Raymond into her arms, and thanked him for showing up when he did. "Let's go out for dinner." Raymond said. She didn't tell him that she had already eaten a bacon and egg sandwich. She and Jody had no plans. She lied to Dawkins. Jody would be late getting home. "Sounds good." She said. "Let's try that barbeque place that Jody told us about." With his arms around her, they left. Raymond didn't mention Dr. Dawkins being at her house when he arrived. Why was he there, he pondered. And was it his first visit? Something went wrong, he concluded. An unhappy experience reflected from both of them.

Raymond and Maria were very quite. She, too, was reminiscing. At the restaurant, Maria said, "I'm sorry to be so speechless. I'll tell you about it later." Raymond muttered, "We both have some issues to talk about." He took her hand and led her into the restaurant.

After they had ordered and been served, they began to chat about family issues. Raymond talked about Jody, what a good worker he was, how dependable he was, and always at work on time. He told her that he had a special feeling for Jody, and had much confidence in him. He told her that Jody talked with their customers about the church. Some of them had actually listened and asked questions about the minister. Jody was very positive on that issue. None of that surprised Maria too much. She had noticed that Jody was becoming a stronger believer. He read his bible nightly, but had only recently begun to do so. She shared that with Raymond. He told her that Allison too, had begun to read the bible. Now with so much peace and calm, they went back to Maria's. There were still some issues to discuss, but that could wait.

As Raymond parked in Maria's yard, she asked him, "Are you coming in, or don't you have time?" He already had his feet on the ground, and answered, "Of course, I'm coming in if you like it or not." Maria slapped him on his shoulder and replied, "Good choice, man." Maria was so elated as they walked into the house. She asked if he would like a glass of tea. He said he did. "Do you know where the kids are tonight?" Raymond asked. "They are probably at the movie." She guessed. "Raymond, you and Allison are still going with us to the Derby, aren't you?" Without any hesitation, he said, "Yes." She hesitated, and then went on," We leave on Monday, you know." Maria told him how happy she was that they were going. She picked up his hand and kissed it. "Are you picking me up for church tomorrow?" He smiled at her, and replied, "Count on it."

At the church the next day, the whole family seemed so happy. Raymond had missed the past two Sundays, and people were wondering if anything was wrong between him and Maria. Paps and Jo couldn't stop grinning. They were so glad that something had apparently been fixed. As soon as the services ended, Pastor Harris came to Raymond, patted his arm and said,"Good to have you back. We missed you. I called you, but you were out. Maria, you look cheerful today." He turned back to Raymond and asked, "Is there anything I can do for you?"

Raymond shook his head, and said,"Not today, but thank you." Several others came to Raymond and said they had missed him. Paps came to Raymond, and asked him, "Who's driving tomorrow?" Raymond hadn't given any thought to it. "Jody, I suppose."Paps said he thought that would be a good choice. Raymond suggested that the four of them meet at Maria's, and he'd pick them up there. Three could ride in the front, and three in the back. He thought that would be better then taking two vehicles. Paps agreed with him. The four of them went to Jo's for lunch. She had already prepared it. "Where are the kids?" Jo wanted to know. Maria looked around, and replied, "I have no idea. They were both here a few minutes ago."

Back at home, Maria had some business to take care of. She was on a two weeks break, but had to drop by the hospital briefly before she left. She typed out a resignation stating that her two weeks vacation would also be her two week notice that she would not return to work. She went to the hospital and turned it in that evening. She did not say anything about Dr. Dawkins, but did state that she had been spoken to in a very degrading manner, by a staff member. She kept this to herself. No one else needed to know right now.

Chapter 6

Monday morning came a bit too soon, but everyone was ready by the time Raymond arrived. He and Allison were cheerful and ready to hit the road. Raymond gave his keys to Jody. "Who appointed me as the driver?" He asked. "I did." Raymond replied. "I didn't know you were my boss on vacation." Jody sneered, and pushed Raymond's shoulder. They started out with three men in the front seat, and three women in the back.

Though a little crowded for some, the trip had a good beginning. The women had more room than the men did. No one complained or grumbled until they stopped for lunch. Jody suggested that everyone change seats. He looked at Raymond and said, "That means that you will be driving." Raymond shook his head, "We're not half way yet. You drive half way, and then I'll take over." As they began to reload to continue their trip, Jody grabbed Allison and pushed her into the front seat. He glanced at Raymond and said, "You figure the rest of it out." Raymond clapped his hands, and said "Thank you." He pushed Maria to the center, and got into the seat beside her. Jo placed a small pillow to the back of her head and went to sleep. Raymond whispered to Maria, "You're not acting right today. Is anything wrong?" She laid her head on his shoulder and whispered back, "Yes. We'll talk about it later." Jody had an eye on them from the rear view mirror. He, too, had been wondering if something was bothering his mom. Paps and Jo had noticed that Maria was not acting quiet right. She was too quiet and appeared to be of nimble mind.

Jody and Allison began singing Jesus Hold My Hand. Jody asked, "Dad, how long before we're half way there?" No answer, Raymond, Maria, and Jo were asleep. Jody and Allison kept singing. No one had heard them sing together. They were good. Eyes began to pop open and the passengers began to move around, and then became alert. Unfinished dreams were forgotten. Raymond asked Jody to stop at the next rest stop and he would take over the driving. That suited Jody. For now he and Allison would move to the back.

At Brannon Mall, he pulled into the parking lot. "We all need a walk." He proclaimed. In the mall, each went his own way, but agreed to meet back at the food court in one hour. Raymond and Maria went in opposite direction from the other four. They walked fast to give their bodies a little work out. They had sit too long. Raymond wanted to ask Maria about her problem, but decided not to. Another time and another place would become available. Was that Dr. Dawkins a part of it? He pondered. They all met back at the food court, and then back on the road. Maria sat up front with Raymond and her Dad, Jody and Allison began updating everyone about the destination for which they were headed.

They explained in detail. Jody began by telling them, though Frankfort is the capital of Kentucky, Louisville is the largest city. He felt sure that everyone who lives in the Bluegrass state, sings My Old Kentucky Home. Goldenrods are the state flower, and the Cardinal is the state bird. Kentucky has two National Parks, the Mammoth Cave near Cave city, and Cumberland Gap near Middlesboro. And, of course, the state is noted for producing championship thoroughbred horses. "Enough, enough." Jo said. "Why don't you two sing some more? I enjoyed your singing together."

At that point, Raymond asked Jody. "And you know all of this because?" Allison picked up, "Dad, did you ever hear about the internet?" Paps answered."I've heard of it, but don't really know what it means." Jody spoke again. "Mom, why don't you get Paps and Granny a computer, teach them what it's for, and how to use it?" Maria said she would think about it. Jody asked if she had gone on line to learn something about the Derby. She had not. "Don't get me a computer until I ask for one." Jo warned. "Paps and I have too many other things to do."

It was time to call it a day. Everyone was tired and Raymond pulled into the motel park. Paps reminded the others, "Dinner is on me tonight. As soon as we're checked in, head for the cafeteria." They pulled tables and chairs together, and the six relaxed with a plate full of food. "We'll be at Churchill Downs before noon tomorrow. Louisville probably has more horses that we can count. I know we'll see some beauties that will awe us." Paps said. Raymond picked up, "You're right. The Derby has a reputation of being the most prestigious horse race in the country. And all are thoroughbred." Jody snickered, "Well, they are not dumb after all." He whispered to Allison.

Jo asked, "How many sitting at this table has ever ridden a horse?" Paps raised his hand, Jo raised her hand. Jody asked,"Paps were your horses stallions, geldings, fillies, studs, mares, or jockeys?" The four older ones burst into laughter. Paps answered. "My horses were stallions, and mares. I was the only jockey."Maria looked at Jody and explained, "A jockey is not a horse. The jockey is the rider." Jody placed both hands over his face and said "Boo Hoo. Shows what I know." Raymond muttered"Really?" "Not my fault." Jody said. "My mom never bought me a horse, neither did my grandparents." Everyone laughed so loud; they got the waiter's attention.

When they had finished eating, they all wandered around the motel lobby. It was large and had some seating space. Jo and Paps went on to their room and made ready for bed. Jody was tired, and went on to his and Maria's room. He needed a shower before she got there. Allison headed for her and Raymond's room. Raymond felt more relaxed than he had all day. He and Maria each took a magazine from a rack, and sat down on the couch. Raymond put his magazine down and turned to Maria. "Can you talk with me now?" She answered, yes, and began to release herself of the secret that had kept her agitated. She explained Dr. Dawkins' visit to her house, the humiliating statements he had made, and that she was throwing him out as Raymond showed up. Raymond said how glad he was that things turned out as they did. He had a feeling, up to that point, that there might be a connection forming between the two. He did realize, however, as he saw Dawkins leaving her house, that something was wrong. Though he felt relieved, he knew that she was very upset. Maria said, "There is one more issue that I haven't told anyone. Yesterday, I took my resignation to the hospital and turned it in. I will not go back to work there." Raymond said he was very proud of her decision. He knew that she could find another job when and if she wanted to. She laughed."What do you mean "if"? No if's about it. I will need a new job soon. Maybe I acted a bit too hasty, but I will not tolerate disrespect from anyone. I know that I'm not better than anyone else, but I am as good. The size house I live in has nothing to do with who or what I am." Raymond agreed with her, and the two of them went to their rooms.

Early Saturday morning they arrived at Churchill Downs, and claimed their seats. As they waited Paps offered a little information before Jody could take over. He explained The Run for the Roses, and told them of one horse who won the Roses, but his owner rejected it because the horse didn't like flowers. Raymond said a blanket with over five hundred roses would sort of scare him. Paps agreed with him. It was Jody's turn. "Are we going to get a Mint Julep?" "What is that?" Jo inquired. Jody was excited. It seemed that he was the only one who knew. "Well, the Mint Julep is a famous drink made of bourbon, mint, and syrup. It's served with ice in a painted glass that has pictures of Derby winners on it." Paps said, "Thank you Jody for that information, but I think you already know whether or not we'll get one. Then Jody told them about Secretariat, a horse that broke a speed record set in 1964, and contained the record for 35 years. Secretariat was also a Triple Crown winner.

The race began. The Barfield's, Reeder's and Marshall's had never been more excited. All of them were talking at the same time, laughing, and slightly screaming. "Which horse did you bet on?" Allison asked her Dad. "None." He responded. They were as amazed at the jockeys as they were the horses. The winner came in. The race ended. They didn't want to leave. Their experiences were unbelievable fantastic. To have seen one of the oldest thoroughbred races the U.S. ran their adrenalin up almost to boiling. "We'll come back next year." Paps promised.

When they left the motel, Raymond headed in what Jody thought was the wrong direction. "Where are you going?" Raymond said, "This is the way I was told to go." Jody laughed."And who told you?"

Raymond replied, "The same one who tells you what to do." Jody looked at Maria. "Where are we going?"She told him, "Frankfort. They have recently replaced the old capitol building, and I want to see it. I also want to go to the horse cemetery to see a horse size bronze statue." Jody and Allison thought that would be a good trip. Paps said that route home would be quicker. Everyone was ready for home. "We'll make brief stops between here and home." Paps said. "Suits me. I put you in charge." They rode around Frankfort viewing the old and new capitol buildings. Then they drove on to the horse cemetery. The bronze statue got everyone's attention. The men, especially, were more impressed. They examined it all the way around, and then from top to bottom. Paps was the designated driver, and he was ready to move on. "Let's stop at Cumbering Falls." Allison asked. "O.K." Paps said. "But that's the last stop." They spent about two hours walking around the falls. All six were glad of the stop. Raymond announced that Kentucky had an altitude from 257 ft. to 4, 145 ft, and a land mileage of near 40,000 sq. miles. Most of his audience said "Uh-huh."

Getting home was terrific. Paps drove on to his house first and then turned the keys over to Raymond. At Maria's Raymond and Allison went in with them. The main reason was to unload their luggage and take it in for her, not that Jody couldn't do it, but it gave Raymond a good excuse to go inside. He wanted a few minutes with Maria. Jody sensed that, and took Allison onto the front porch and started swinging. Raymond took Maria into his arms. He held her close rubbing the top of her head with his chin."Your greatest achievement is still with you. You have your son and all the accomplishments the two of you have acquired. You have loving and caring parents, and you have me. So what is there to worry about? You are a positive person filled with determination. So smile and let all that other stuff die." Raymond didn't know what to do, but he knew she would snap out of her dilemma soon. Maria was silent. "You need to talk with your parents and Jody." Maria freed herself from Raymond's tight hold, and placed her arms around him. She whispered," Thank you. I will." Raymond said "Go to bed. Tomorrow will be a better day .A rainbow will shine." He went out the door and told Allison to jump into the truck. Jody went inside immediately. He kissed his Mom's cheek and said, "Good night-good dreams." He went on to his room. "Maybe we can talk at the breakfast table in the morning," He yelled.

Maria got up early. She felt fine. She asked God to give her peace and quiet, and He did. A rainbow glowed. She was making pancakes when Jody entered the kitchen. As soon as the syrup was pored over the pancakes, Jody began. "Mom, please tell me what is bothering you. Are you sick?" Maria assured him that she was not sick. Then she explained the experience with Dr. Dawkins, and that she had resigned from her job. Jody was upset. "I wish I had been here, I'd have thrown him out properly, and knocked him flat on his butt off the porch." Maria said a fight was not needed. Jody added, "Well, why did you resign instead of getting him fired?" Maria answered, "That would have been hard to do. And it might keep me from finding another job." Jody said, "Mom, have you told Granny and Paps?" Maria told him that she had only, yesterday, shared it with Raymond, but no one else. "Raymond said I made the right decision." Now, I have to get over it, and move on. I have prayed about it." Jody smiled, "So have I. Not knowing what was wrong, and knowing that something was, I prayed that God would bless you in whatever way was best for you." Tears filled Maria's eyes. She thanked Jody and told him that a prayer for someone is the best we can do.

After Jody went to work, Maria went to her parents. She shared everything with them, and asked them not to be up set, she'd have another job soon. Paps was teetering on the edge of going to the hospital. "That man needs to be expunged from the face of the earth." he said. Jo took his arm and asked him to relax. Paps kept on, "That man is a shinning example of a nobody. His greatest achievements are probably behind him." Jo calmed him down, and told him."Don't let this man get you down, If you do, you're letting him control you, and he is not worthy of that. Stay in control of yourself." She turned to Maria "Don't let your decisions have anything to do with him. You decide which way you are going, how you will get there, and what you will do." She added. "Always ask yourself why, and let your answer always be –because I want to, NOT because of anyone else." Maria placed both arms around her Mom, then she hugged her Dad. "I'm so very proud of each of you." Maria went home a different person. She was her old self again. She would handle future decisions.

Raymond picked Maria up for church the next morning. He noticed she was calm, happy, and laughing. He began smiling too. What a rainbow! Just as they pulled into the parking lot, Jody and Allison pulled in behind them. The four walked in together, and, though unusual, they all sat together. Jo and Paps were over in the next isle, but they came over and sat with them. Jody knew, without asking, that his Mom and her parents had talked. Pastor Harris motioned for Jody. Jody got up and went to the alter where the pastor stood. They had a brief talk before Jody returned to his seat. Now, Maria, as well as the others, wondered what that was about. It didn't take too long to find out. The piano was playing, the choir was singing, then the assistant pastor announced that Jody and Allison would sing a duet together. Everyone was surprised, but Maria could not speak. She glanced at Raymond and tried to smile, but his lips were trembling, and he couldn't speak or smile either. They clasp hands and squeezed tight. The piano began. Jody and Allison stood onstage, and sang "When the Roll is Called up Yonder, I'll be there." Maria and Raymond had to wipe their eyes. When the singing was over, Maria softly voiced, "Amen." And so did the rest of the congregation.

After church the six went to Jo's and Paps' for dinner. As usual, Jo had a plan. She had baked a ham, and three casseroles. After they had finished eating, Jo went to the kitchen. She asked Maria and Allison to clean off the table. Everyone was expecting something. Jo came back to the dinning area with a huge cake. She placed it on the table and lit twenty candles. "Make a wish, then blow them out with one breath." She said to Jody. They all sang Happy Birthday. After Jody caught his breath, he said, "On my next birthday put two candles on one side and one on the other." Jo said, "But that's just three." Jody laughed at her and remarked, "Granny, two and one is twenty one. Then I won't loose my breath blowing out candles." Paps came in with a basket of gifts cards. Most of the cards contained a gift card. Jody grabbed Allison and they danced around the room. Jo put on a CD, and all six of them danced. Jo thought it was time for a little praise. "Jody and Allison, you were absolutely great singing that duet this morning. And I loved that old song. Everyone agreed by expressing their own personal views. Jody was most excited "We'll do it again soon." He said.

Monday morning was no paradise. Jody had to be at work early. In fact, he got to work before Raymond did, which was unusual. Jody had keys to the business, and he knew how to unlock the doors. Raymond pondered as he stopped at Maria's. She was typing her resume when he arrived. Just who she would send it to, she didn't have a clue. Raymond asked her not to push the idea. He wanted her to give it a couple of weeks. She wouldn't starve as long as the others were working. He had already given Jody a nice raise, but Maria did not know it. "I've already had two weeks off, and I can't just sit on my butt and wait. I have to get busy finding my way. No telling how long it will take me to get another job. Nurses are not hired around every corner." "Who will you send your first resume to?" Raymond asked. "I will send one to the other two hospitals." Raymond kept quiet. She had already made her decision. Raymond needed a secretary and a bookkeeper, but he'd put that on hold right now.

That night Jody said, "Mom, we need a secretary and a bookkeeper. I know you could do that." "Good, I may have to." She answered. "It wouldn't be a bad job." Jody assured her. So, he and Raymond had already discussed the matter, she concluded. You really enjoy working with Raymond, don't you?" He said he liked working with Raymond, and that he had a love for him. Maria mused for a moment, and asked, "What kind of love?" He was silent for a minute, then began,"Raymond is sort of like a Dad to me, something I never had. I trust him, I confide in him, and he is honest with me, even when he disagrees. If I ask him a personal question, he'll give me an answer. If I ask him a question that's none of my business, however, he'll let me know." Maria was in shock! "I never knew the two of you had such a personal relationship. I thought Paps answered your questions." Jody glanced at her and said,"Sometimes we need someone outside the family to give us unbiased opinions. At my age, when I ask a question, I need a straight forward honest answer regardless to circumstances. I have shared some personal opinions with Raymond, and I know the information is safe and secret. Maria managed to speak. "I guess you know you just tossed a snowball that smashed right in my face?"Jody laughed."I have enjoyed our talk and went to his room.

Chapter 7

Jody sat on the edge of his bed and thought about his future. One never knows what lies ahead, no matter what direction they are traveling. He had finished two years of college, and had completed all the basics. He had made good grades, but wasn't sure he wanted to pursue a medical degree. There were a number of other areas he was interested in, but then, he'd think of Paps. Paps was paying his college expenses, but did that mean that Paps controlled him? No, he decided. If he didn't take control of his own decisions, he'd never be a man. Paps wouldn't stop supporting him. Even if he wanted to, Granny wouldn't let him. So that would give him a solid foundation. After all, his Mom was their only child and he as their only grandchild. Of course, they would support him, no matter which way he took off. Maybe if he had a good talk with Pastor Harris, he could help him.

Jody made an appointment with Pastor Harris the next evening. He got off work at six, and met with him at seven. Jody called his Mom to let her know that he would be late getting home. She did not question him, but concluded he and Raymond were working late. When Jody sat facing Pastor Harris, he didn't know what to say or where to start. "What's on your mind?" The Pastor asked. "I don't want to be a medical doctor. I want to be a preacher." The Pastor patted his shoulder and said. "I know." There was silence, then the Pastor broke it. "Jody, you are a very smart young man. You are a good Christian, and you can become a minister if you so desire. All it takes is strong desire and determination. If you have that, you will achieve your aim. It's determination that makes dreams come true." Jody left feeling more at peace than he had for awhile. The next bridge to cross would be telling his family, but he would. One thing for sure, his decision had been made, and he would fuel it with accomplishment.

Raymond found Maria's door open, and walked on in. She was in the kitchen making vegetable soup. "So, you worked late?" He said he did not work late, just late getting to her house. She wondered why Jody was working late, if Raymond wasn't. Something was not right. A few minutes later, Jody came home. He realized, seeing Raymond there that Maria already knew that he didn't work late. She put the food on the table, and the three of them sat down to eat. It was so obvious to Maria and Raymond that Jody had a secret that was about to be exposed. The door bell rang, then Jo and Paps came in. Both Jody and Maria were in great wonder. Why did they come at this time? Maria poured them a bowl of soup. Jo had brought a peach cobbler.

During the meal, Paps spoke to Jody. "So, you are pulling out of the medical field? At least, that's what I heard." Then Jo added. "It's a field that both your grandparents and your Mother choose, and stayed with it why not you?" Jody couldn't think or speak. He had been silenced by surprise. How did they know? He wondered. Raymond spoke for him. "It's perfectly normal for anyone, especially a young person, to make a number of new plans before the age of twenty-five. At age twenty, however, one usually thinks his final decision is made, but it seldom is. Jody has talked with me about this, and I honestly think the final decision belongs to him. And I know, whatever it is, his choice will be right for him. So, I will personally endorse his decision." Paps and Jo gave Raymond a very weird look, before anyone else could speak; Maria spoke, "Thank you Raymond. I agree with you. What Jody does next, is entirely up to him, and he will have my support. He has talked with me about this matter, and I totally approve. He doesn't have to follow anyone's footsteps; he is qualified to start his own path."

Jody finally started breathing again, and said, "Thank you Mom. Thank you Raymond. I'm sorry if I have disappointed anyone, but I've been thinking about this for a while, and have talked with a number of people who knows what I'm talking about, and respects my decision. Pastor Harris has been a great help to me and I greatly appreciate his understanding. I will be going to Atlanta Christian College in the fall, and my aim is to become a minister." He turned to his grandparents, and said, "I was planning to talk with you about this." He smiled at them and asked, "How did you know?" Jo answered that Allison had mentioned that she and Jody were changing directions. She did not mention the Christian College. Everyone appeared pleased. Paps said, "I am very happy for you. You can still count on us." Jo was crying with joy. "You'll make a fine minister," She whispered.

Jody had a meeting to attend. Jo and Paps needed their nap. Maria and Raymond were left alone. As Raymond placed his arms around her, she began crying. She finally kissed him on the cheek, and said, "This is the best day I have had in quiet awhile. I am so happy." Raymond replied, "And is that why you're crying?" He pulled her closer to him. She laughed, and said, "I really don't know why I'm crying, with joy, I suppose. You will never know how much I appreciate the support you gave Jody. I was afraid there was going to be a riffle." Raymond said, "Me too. That's why I spoke up before your parents could say anything more." He looked at her straight in the face and added, "I want you to know I was prepared to give Jody whatever financial support he might need, and I still am. I will not, however, get into your parent's way." Maria said, "Thank you. Let's go to the mall and browse around for awhile. We need a walk."

Neither Jody nor Allison would be coming home every night, now that they were both in Atlanta. It would be convenient, however for them to come home on week ends. Maria's house was too quiet. The walls echoed silence. Raymond dropped by often, he too, was experiencing a shade of loneliness. They ate together on a daily bases. Raymond was overly concerned about Maria. He wanted to be there for her on any occasion or situation she may find difficult. They visited Paps and Jo regularly. They too missed Jody.

Maria stopped by Raymond's. She wanted to see his paintings. Did he paint them? They never talked about it. How strange! She was going to ask questions. He had said once that he was a dabbler. Why hadn't she shown some interest? She walked up to the paintings hanging on the living room and dinning room walls. Raymond was observing her. "Raymond, did you do all this painting?" He glanced at her and wondered if she was blind, then said, "Whose name is on them?" She felt a bit ignorant. On each painting was Raymond's name on the lower right hand corner. Maria was amazed. "When did you paint?" He mumbled,"Years ago." Maria sat down beside him, and excitedly asked,"Why aren't you still painting?" "I lost interest, and I don't have time." She sensed a bit of sadness, then asked,"Could you teach me?" Raymond laughed. "A teacher, I am not," She had definitely lighted a spark in his thinking. He began, "Anyone can paint, if they want to. Desire, however, is a must. If you want to paint, you can. If you don't really care about it, you can't." Maria said. "I want you to lead me," Raymond laughed. "When I say you can paint, I absolutely believe it. I would not have thought so a few years ago, but starting to paint with absolutely no background for it, and after selling most of my paintings, I know anyone can do it who really has a desire for it. It gave me a lot of fun ad pleasure at a time when I needed it. A friend of mine, who is a true artist, encouraged me. He set up classed for me, and nothing delighted me more than a finished piece of work. One thing to keep in mind is that God, the great Universal Creator, never duplicated anything, and neither will you. It is impossible for me to paint two roses, rivers, or two of anything exactly alike. So your paintings will be unique." Maria was very interested. "How can I get started?" Raymond knew Maria needed something to fill the loneliness that surrounded her and her house. He was going through the same thing. "I'll get you set up with a good teacher. A few painting classed will push your interest."

Maria couldn't believe she was actually dabbling oil paint on a canvas. The instructor was very friendly, and knew what she was doing. Don't place limitations on yourself. It's not fair. You can do more than you think. Soon you will discover a new you." Maria soon finished her first painting, but wasn't sure she liked it. It didn't look like the others. Then she recalled what Raymond had told her. The instructor noticed that no one was really pleased. She told them. "Who can say that yours are better than hers, or that hers is better than yours? They are as individual as we are. Both are good. My yellow rose doesn't look like hers, but it does look like a yellow rose, and that was my only endeavor." Maria began to feel better. She took her rose to Raymond. He went on and on about how beautiful it was, and so realistic too.

Marie took her rose to show her parents. They were both mesmerized. They were as excited as Raymond on the excellent job she had doe. Jo shared a truth she had read. "Green goes with all colors. If you don't think so, look at a flower garden." Jo was too excited. "I think I'll take some art classes. I always wanted to paint on canvas, but never had time." Paps quickly answered, "Well, you have time now, so get started. It's time for both of us to get out of the house and do something." Maria couldn't believe what she was hearing, but was so pleased. She made arrangements for Jo to begin classes the following week.

Paps got a part time job at a local hospital, and that freed Jo. Maria's next assignment was a vase of different flowers. She didn't have time to miss Jody. She was always excited about the changes on the canvas. She explained to her mother that no two paintings would look exactly alike, even if the same artist painted them. "No one could paint Mona Lisa like Leonardo da Vince did and he couldn't paint her to look like one that I painted." They both laughed. Jo said, "Thank you my darling daughter, for getting me into this. Even your Dad, is happy about it." Maria asked, "How does Dad like his job?" Jo said that he loved working in the ER.

Chapter 8

Maria was snoozing on the couch when the phone rang. Who could that be, she had just talked with her Mom and to Raymond before she lay down. She jumped up and ran to the phone. It had to be Jody, but it was not his voice that said, "Maria, is there any way you could come back to work? We really need you. Two nurses and a doctor have left. Please, please, come back." Maria couldn't believe what she was hearing. "Yes. When?" She said. "Tomorrow morning, if possible." Without any hesitation, Maria replied. "I'll be there." Since her painting classes were scheduled for late evening, she could handle both obligations. She called her Mom, bubbling over with the good news. Jo was excited about it."But, you still have to stay with your painting classed."Jo reminded her. Maria assured her that she would hang on to that. She called Raymond and asked him to drop by on his way home from work. "I'm fixing you a good dinner." She told him.

Raymond left immediately. He knew something was going on. What he pondered. He hoped it had nothing to do with Jody or Allison. Was there anything going on with Maria that he didn't know about? Maybe it was her parents. He jumped into his truck and took off. Maria was surprised when he showed up so early. "You're earlier than I expected. I just got to the kitchen myself." Raymond responded, "Not much going on at the shop, so I decided to come on. When you said you were cooking, I began to smell something good, so I left."

As they sat down to eat, Raymond said, "O.K., tell me about it." Maria smiled, and asked, "About what?" Raymond said, "You know what." Then she began telling him about the phone call. "I am so excited." She said. Raymond was still wondering."Is Dawkins still there?" "I don't think so. That's why they called me. I didn't ask any questions. I am also wondering who the two nurses are that left. I'll find out after I go back." Raymond was wondering if Paps had anything to do with this. He was not at the same hospital, but he probably had his foot in this situation. He didn't want to mention that to Maria, but he had a burning desire to find out. Sure, he was in on it. He probably managed to get Dawkins fired. One thing for sure, Maria had a strong family. Each one of them stood ready to defend each other. As Raymond was about to leave, he turned to Maria and asked, "Do you want me to pick you up in the morning and drive you to work?" Maria smirked at him, "No. I have a car and know how to drive it."

Maria was too excited that morning as she left for work. She loved her job, but more than that, she loved her pay check. She had been offered an acceptable raise, and felt that she was back on track. She was anxious to find out what changes had been made. Who was in charge of the birthing center, surely not Dawkins? She pulled into the parking lot, ran into the hospital, and was greeted by several friends. She also got a few hugs. She laughed and appeared to be happy to see everyone. Finally, she asked one of the nurses, "Where is Dr. Dawkins?" The nurse said, "He is no longer here. He took a job offer from St. Louis." Maria pondered, then said, "He must have been looking for a change."The nurse whispered. "I don't think he had a choice." Now, Maria was really wondering. As she began to settle down, "Thank you God." She whispered, and went on duty.

Maria and Jo met that evening at art class. Maria shared her entire day with her Mom. Jo was almost as excited as Maria was when Maria told her that Dr .Dawkins had taken another job. Jo didn't act surprised. Then Maria, like Raymond, began to wonder if Paps was in some way responsible. After class, Maria went home with Jo. Paps was there. He'd just arrived as they walked in. Paps hugged Maria, and said, "I'm glad our schedules seem to work perfectly. By the time I get home, you two are here. And I'm real glad that you two have a good schedule. How are things in the birthing center now?" Maria thought, yes, he does know and I haven't told him. How did he know? What did he do? Surely, he did something. No doubt about it. "I'm waiting for an answer." Paps said. Maria replied, "Well, today being my first day back, everything seemed normal. I enjoyed it as I usually have." "Dr. Dawkins wasn't there, was he?"Maria was quiet for a minute, "No, I don't think so. He must have been off today". Paps assured her, "I don't think you'll be seeing him again. He's gone for good."

Jody called to say he'd be home for the week end. Allison would be coming with him. Maria forgot everything else. She was anxious to see her son, and to show him her paintings. She would bake a ham and a large cake. She called her parents to invite them for dinner on Saturday night. She called Raymond to tell him the good news. He and Allison would also eat diner with them. Raymond came as soon as they hung up the phone. There were some more things he wanted to know. She told him about her talk with her parents. They both agreed that Paps was, in someway, involved in Dr. Dawkins leaving the hospital. Raymond suggested that they should not bring up the subject again. If Paps wants to expose himself, let him. "We both know that Paps had something to do with it. We just don't know how, and we don't need to know. So don't worry about it and do your work without concern."Raymond told her. Maria promised she would not mention it again, nor give it too much thought.

Jody was so glad to be home. It had been almost a month since he left. Maria had thought he would be home ever week end, but apparently it was not his plan. He loved the Christian College, and was very glad of that decision. At dinner that night, Jody did most of the talking, and everyone else respectfully listened. He was taking courses in the New Testament and the Old Testament. He was also taking a course in biblical history. He explained all this, and spoke of his teachers. He was also teaching a Sunday school class at the church that he and Allison attended. He and Allison sang together often, and both were choir members. He had made friends with the Pastor, and really enjoyed his sermons. He called Pastor Harris and shared his church involvement with him. Paps and Jo expressed their appreciation of Jody's decision. They were very proud of him, and let him know it.

Allison was quieter than usual, but then, Jody didn't give her much of a chance to talk. Maria asked her a few questions, and she did answer. Marie was sitting by Raymond. She placed her hand on his leg and patted it. He too, noticed Allison's silence. Allison was taking four courses, which kept her busy. She was making good grades, and happy to be in math education. Raymond said it was time to go. As he and Allison neared the door, Maria took Allison into her arms. She held her close, kissed her cheek, and said, "Don't forget that I love you. You're the only daughter I have. If you ever need me, let me know." Raymond noticed Maria's affection, and headed out the door. Jo and Paps didn't stay much longer before they went home.

Maria and Jody needed some time alone before he left. Maria showed him her paintings, and told him about her and Jo's classes together. He was amazed that she was painting. He was also very glad that she was enjoying her spare time. More than that, he was happy that she had her job back. Paps was a trooper, he already knew that. Maria asked him about Allison. Jody said "OK, don't let anyone know that I told you, especially Granny. Allison had a boy friend that she seemed to think a lot of. She doesn't want Raymond to know right now. They have some classes together, and have gone out a few times. I've not met him, and all I know is what Allison has shared with me." Maria mused that for a moment, then asked, "How do you feel about her having a boy friend?" Jody stated that it didn't bother him at all. He said they were like brother and sister. He loved Allison, but not as a sweetheart, more like a best friend or a sister. He said she felt the same way about him. They both loved each other, but were not in love. Maria yawned, and they both went to bed.

Sunday morning Raymond and Allison picked them up, and off to church they went. Pastor Harris was so glad to see Jody and Allison. He mentioned to the audience that some important members had returned. He asked them to stand as he explained why they had not been in church lately. After the services, the six went to a new restaurant that had recently opened. Jody invited the pastor and Tonya to go eat with them. Tonya was a most caring and loving person. She hugged Jody and Allison, and told them how proud she was of both of them. That lady would do anything she could for anyone. When they had finished eating, Jody and Allison said good bye, and left for Atlanta.

Raymond took Maria home, and asked."What are we going to do the rest of the day?" "Let's go to a movie." She pleaded. "We don't need to go home right now." She added. Raymond laughed,"Agree." The movie was about a couple who had been dating for a couple of years, but never mentioned marriage. Finally, at the end, they became engaged. The audience applauded. "About time." Some of them yelled. Everybody was laughing with joy. On the way home, Raymond asked,"How did you like the movie?" Maria's brain had been reminiscing. "I loved it. It didn't look like they'd ever get together." Raymond said, "Reminds me of a couple I know."He went on in the house with Maria, and she poured each of them a glass of iced tea.

They sipped and sipped before Raymond asked, "Are we ever going to get married?" Maria replied,"Not before you ask me." They both laughed. Raymond slipped over nearer to her, placed an arm around her, and said "Maria, you know I love you with all my heart, body, and soul. There is nothing that I wouldn't do for you. I also love your son." He reached over to kiss her and to wipe away her tears. "Will you please marry me?" He pulled a handkerchief from his pocket and handed it to her. She wiped her face, kissed him, and said,"Of course, I will." He kissed her again, and asked, "When?" She replied, "Tomorrow morning, early, so we can get to work on time. In that case, it will have to be before eight o'clock." They embraced, and decided to make that decision tomorrow. Raymond pulled a ring from his pocket, and placed it on Maria's finger. She was so surprised. "How long have you had this?" Raymond said,"About a year."

Maria went to bed thinking about Jody and Allison. She was sure both of them would be so happy to know that she and Raymond were engaged. Jody would be very excited. He had already expressed a love for Raymond, and Raymond surely loved him. Her parents would be awed. She would not mention this to anyone until a date had been set. When? Where? How? She couldn't come up with answers. Let Raymond do it. Her hands were full with her painting projects, not to mention, of course, her job. When would she have time for Raymond? He would be getting off from work about the time her art classed started. Oh well, he already knew that, so let him figure it out. She wanted to make the wedding simple. Yes, it would be her first marriage, but at her age, simplicity was more appreciated. Her Mom would surely want her to wear a long dress, dragging the floor behind her, a long wide veil, a new hair do, and no telling what else. She would make her own decisions, and would dress as she always had on Sunday Morning. Decision made, she went to sleep.

At work that morning, it was quiet obvious that something was going on with Maria. Her fellow workers noticed she was too quiet. Finally, they began noticing the ring, Maria was lambasted with questions. She told everyone that she'd let them know as soon as she did. They all knew Raymond. He came to the birthing center often to have lunch with Maria. Those who had met him liked him. Some had even had lunch with him and Maria.

When she got home that afternoon, she called Jody. He, like everyone else, wanted to know when. "It sure took you two a long time. You have obviously been in love for at least a year." Maria mused,"How did you know?" Jody snickered, "Who didn't?" Then he added."Mom, I am really so glad for you. As soon as a time is set, call me immediately. Should I tell Allison, or should I wait for her Dad to tell her? Maria said it would be best if she heard it from Raymond. Maria was attempted to go tell her parents, but wasn't quiet sure she was ready for that. She couldn't wait. She called them and told Jo the good news. Jo went on and on with instructions on how everything would be. Maria quickly said, "Mom, I've got to hang up and run to the bath room." She hung up the phone and went to the kitchen. After pouring a glass of tea for her self, the door bell rang. Maria was tempted not to answer it, but did.

Jo and Paps rushed into the house. Jo began,"Tell me all about it." Maria said, "Mom, I have already told you all that I know. You'll just have to wait until I know more. Paps said, "Call Jody, he needs to know about this." Maria gave him a strange look and said,"He was the first one I called." Jo began. "Well, you must get married in the church, and let your Dad escort you down the isle. You'll have to wear a long white dress covered in lace. I'll get it for you. Let's go to the mall tomorrow and look around. What kind of shoes do you want?" "Mom," Maria cut her off. "Let's don't make any plans right now. The truth is, I don't know what I want, But Raymond and I will decide." Jo could see that Maria was a bit too upset. She sympathized with her, and told Paps they should go. As soon as they had left, Maria lay on the couch. She loved her Mom very much, but at times, she got on her nerves.

Raymond went to the hospital to have lunch with Maria, but as he walked into the birthing center, at least five women rushed to him. They were laughing and talking, hugging him, and congratulating him. Maria saw this and said, "Turn him loose, he's mine." Lunch was not what Raymond had expected. All five of the ladies ate with them. Before they had finished, a man walked over to them. He offered his hand to Raymond, "I'm Dr. Jose Morris. Congratulations, I think you have made a good choice. It would be hard to run this birthing center, without Maria. I hope she's a good cook." Raymond shook his hand, thanked him, and assured him he was indeed making a wise choice. He also stated that Maria was an excellent cook. Maria was much impressed. She had already told everyone that a date had not been set, and asked them not to mention a date to Raymond. They didn't.

That night Raymond asked Maria, "Let's decide which house we will live in. We will live in the same house, want we?" She slapped his knee."Well, we can live here in my house until Jody needs it, if he ever does. I want Allison to have your house. She may need it after she graduates. In any case, I want her to have your house. I don't want it." He grabbed her and squeezed her hard. "I just want to do whatever you wish." he said. She told him that her parents already had Jody on their deeds, and their house would some day belong to him. She also had Jody listed on her deeds. Raymond said he had no problem with that. She explained that Paps had bought her house and put it her name and Jody's. Raymond understood. He explained that he would keep his house in his name, for a few more years, but already had Allison listed on his will. So she was covered. She may never need it, he thought. That would depend on where she chooses to live after graduation. His guess was, she'd get a teaching job in Atlanta, and stay there. One never knows.

Have you decided on a date yet?" Raymond asked. "It's your choice. He added. Maria said, "I was thinking about waiting until the kids come home again. We'll tell them and no one else, and will get married at the church on Sunday morning as a total surprise to everyone, except the kids. What about that?" Raymond said that sounded good to him."Call the kids and tell them to come home this weekend." He said. Maria laughed and inquired,"That soon"? "Why not"? Raymond said. They decided to call Jody and Allison, tell them, and see when it would be convenient for both of them to come. In the meantime, Raymond would speak with Pastor Harris about their plan."Your parents will go crazy if you don't tell them." Raymond informed her. Maria's response was,"That's exactly what they did, and I never heard of anyone going crazy. Anyway, that's their problem. I like this idea." Raymond assured her that it suited him.

Before Maria went to bed, she called Jody and told him of the present plan. He was sure he would be free, not this week end, but the next one. She told him to let Raymond tell Allison before he mentioned it to her. Allison would surely let him know as soon as she found out. Maris told him that Raymond would call her tonight. "Mom, is week after next good for you?" She told him it would be a great time for her. He promised to call her back the next day. "What does Granny and Paps think about your quick and simple plan"? She assured him that they did not know, and was not going to, until the wedding took place. Jody was so pleased that his Mom had included him in her plans from day one. "Mom, I want to stand beside you during the ceremony. Allison can stand beside her Dad. That will be acceptable, will it not?" Maria could barely speak."I wouldn't have it any other way." She managed to say.

At work the next morning, Maria was so excited; her friends approached her wanting to know if a date had been set. Then she began to think. She would like for her friends to go, but they would have to be at the church, and none of them attended her church. So, that was their problem. They would have to attend that particular Sunday, if they wanted to witness the connection. She'd talk with Raymond about that. She did, however, have a couple of friends that she could trust to keep a lid on her secret. She'd tell them at lunch that day. Raymond would not be there, and she was free to talk. She shared her secret, and they promised to be there. Afterwards, she and Raymond would take family and friends out to lunch. Her friends said lunch would be on them. Reservations would have to be made, in a private room if possible. Maria shared the plan with Raymond that night. He was pleased with it.

Raymond had talked with Allison, and she was most excited about their plan. She would be coming with Jody. Raymond had already talked with the pastor, and he was also excited. He would not mention it until the time to join them as husband and wife. He too, had been expecting this union for along time. Maria and Raymond, for the first time in a long time, felt more relaxed and calm. Maria did more painting that evening than she had in a while. Under no circumstances was she going to wean away from her art classes. She was learning more than she had expected. Raymond shared his engagement with his employees. They, too, was well pleased. One asked him, "Should we now call you Mr. Barfield, or keep calling you Raymond"? Raymond laughed and said, "Whatever floats your bubble."

Chapter 9

Maria was a bit nervous at church that Sunday, and so was Raymond. Maria didn't know one word the pastor said. She was in a trance. One week from today. She was thinking, would change her life. Nothing will ever again be the same. Even when Jody comes home, things will be different. She would still have her freedom to make choices, but total freedom would no longer exist. There were going to be obligations that she'd never known. There would also be different schedules, particularly in the kitchen. Was she ready for all of this? Raymond took her hand and stood up, pulling on her. The church services had ended, and she did not know it. Pastor Harris patted them on the back as they were leaving, and said,"See you two next Sunday."

Jody called and said he and Allison were half way home. Raymond hung out at Maria's until bed time, and then went home. Allison was getting out of Jody's truck as Raymond was pulling into his driveway. They both ran and hugged him, then Jody drove on home. Maria was waiting up for him. Jody embraced her, and was somewhat excited. Maria fixed some hot cocoa, and they sat down at the table. Jody was full of questions, but was not too prompt in asking them. Maria sensed that, and asked, "Is there anything you want to ask me, if so, go ahead." Jody was silent, than asked," "Did you ever tell your parents about your wedding tomorrow? If you didn't, they could be very up set with you." Maria said, "No. I did not tell them. I had rather they didn't get involved. That way, it will be over with by the time they catch their breath." Jody laughed and said, "Well, they gave everyone a shock and surprise, didn't they? So, you and Raymond are doing exactly the same thing." Allison called to tell Maria that she loved her, and sorry that it was too late to drop by.

Jody had another question. "Where are you two going on your honeymoon?" Maria asked, "Are you sure you won't tell anyone?" He nodded his head. "We're going to the cabin for a couple of days, then we'll take the camper through the Smokey Mountains." Jody had yet another question. "That will take how many days?" Maria told him, "We will be gone seven days." Jody asked if she would keep in ouch with him on a daily basis. In case of an accident, or a change in plans, for any reason, he'd need to know. Maria assured her son that she would, as usual, stay in touch. Maybe not daily, but ever couple of days at least. Jody had a feeling that he was loosing his Mom. That it would be her and Raymond from now on, and he would, somehow, not be in the picture. Maria was aware of his feelings. She took him into her arms and assured him he would forever be in her heart. They went to bed. Tomorrow was the big day.

Sunday morning early, Raymond and Allison dropped by. The four would go in two vehicles. Raymond and Jody loaded Maria's luggage into Raymond's truck. Maria put on her favorite dress, one she had worn before, fixed her hair, and was ready to go. Allison assured her that she was beautiful, and that she loved her light blue dress. Raymond wore a beautiful blue dress shirt and tie, but no coat. Men in the church were not wearing suits. Why should he? A suit had nothing to do with what kind of man he was. Jody and Allison would be headed back to Atlanta as soon as they ate lunch. Everyone at church that morning acted normal. It was obvious that no one had a clue. Jo and Paps were already there when the four arrived. They greeted each other and chatted briefly. Jo noticed that Jody was wearing a tie too, how unusual to see him in a tie. Jody patted her on her back, took Allison's arm and they took their seats. Pastor Harris glanced at them and smiled.

Maria noticed two huge flowerpots filled with roses. She whispered to Raymond about it. Raymond had ordered the roses. Just before the service began, some one pulled Maria's ear. She turned around and there were five of her co-workers. Maria hoped her Mom was not noticing that. Jo would not recognize them, of course, but might find it strange. It didn't matter now, the services had begun. Neither Maria nor Raymond was the least bit nervous.

After the sermon was finished, Pastor Harris asked the congregation to give him a few minutes before they got up to leave. "We have a great surprise for you." He announced. Maria did not look toward her parents. Surely, her Mom had figured it out. Pastor Harris asked, "Will Raymond and Maria, Jody and Allison, step forward?" Everyone else, please keep your seat." The four got up and walked to the alter. Jody stood by his Mom, and Allison stood by her Dad. Raymond had one arm around Maria. Jo had both hands over her face. Maria's friends from the hospital were smiling from ear to ear. Three of Raymond's employees were there, and were smiling at him. As soon as they both had said "I do," The pastor dismissed the crowd. Jody went to his grandparents and told them they would have lunch at Country Home Restaurant in a private room. Maria went and greeted her parents, and then left with Raymond.

At the restaurant, about twenty five friends and family met. Everyone was happily cheering. Jo and Paps were as excited as the rest."I had a feeling it might happen just as it did today." Maria embraced her Mom and said." Well, I had a good teacher." Paps said,"You sure did. You followed our steps." Maria was calm. Her friends entertained Raymond. They asked him questions about Maria in a joking manner. Could she cook, or would she have time now that she was an artist. They promised to send him a sandwich ever evening, just in case. He laughed and said he'd let them know. Maria asked them to send two sandwiches, then maybe, she wouldn't have to cook. Pastor Harris talked with Jody about his college involvements. Tonya gave much of her attention to Allison. The pastor seemed to be very pleased with Jody. Raymond had introduced his daughter to Maria's friends, and they talked and laughed with her. "So, you're going to be a math teacher. That's good. We certainly need some people who can add two and two and come up with four. Many obviously can't." Allison said at times she had a problem with that. Jody began talking with his Dad's friends. He knew them, for he had worked with them. They expressed their sympathy that now he would really take orders from Raymond. "Are you kidding? There is no way I'll take orders from him. He will now take orders from me, both him and Mom."e will now take orders fromme. BothhimandMom."

The waitress brought the bill, and was handing it to Raymond. Paps reached over to get it, as the pastor grabbed it. "My gift to you." Jody and Allison had to leave. They had a long way to drive. Maria's friends began to depart. Raymond's friends left, assuring him they would take care of the business until his return. The pastor and Tonya left. Jo and Paps left without asking any questions. Jo said,"Call me when you can." Maria told her that it would be a week. Maria said."Well they have all left us. I guess that means it's our time to go." Raymond and Maria went on to the cabin. They talked about the day. Raymond told her that Allison had a boy friend. She already knew that, but didn't say anything about that. He said that he had thought Allison and Jody would connect. He had hoped they would. Maria said that they might, even yet. Allison may have many boyfriends, before she finds that special one. Same for Jody.

She told him that their children were now brother and sister, and best friends, and that was all for now.

After two days at the cabin, they packed the camper and headed for the Mountains. They had planned this trip several times before, but didn't make it because of a bed shortage for four. This time it would be different. There was plenty of room for two. Maria took her camera. She would take some pictures to paint, and there would be countless scenes to choose from. She loved to paint water, and there were more bubbling streams than she had imagined. She even got a picture of a black bear running toward Raymond as he was running back toward the camper. The flash of the camera caused the bear to change directions. She would have that enlarged to hang in her living room. The kids had to see that. She would also take a copy of it to work. Those girls would really tease Raymond about running from the bear.

In Gatlinburg, they were totally unprepared for the scenic views. They saw Houses on top of high mountains to where no road appeared to lead. Surely, there was a road, but how does one drive straight up? They went through the aquarium, and were unprepared for the massive space with all kinds of sea animals swimming all around. Turning around a curve, Maria almost screamed as a huge shark almost got her head in it's mouth. Raymond put his arms around her. "Don't worry, they can't get you." She said,"Well, that one almost did." They would never forget that visit with thousands of exotic sea creatures. Raymond was interested in the Sky Lift and Aerial Tramway to Alpine slide. Maria went with him, but not excitedly so. She was a bit afraid of heights. Raymond promised to hold on to her. They both enjoyed the spectacular views on the sky lift. They visited a wax museum, and found that to be amazing. Christ in the Smokiest, a life size scene of the story of Christ, in life size figures was most amazing to both Raymond and Maria. The ghost shows, they avoided.

The most pleasure they claimed was the camping. The campsites were in great locations throughout the trip. They walked around the areas observing the water falls, bubbling springs, and the awesome landscape. Maria took pictures of everything. She took pictures of Raymond, and he took pictures of her. They drove on to Cherokee, and stayed over night. They visited the Gambling Casino, but did not gamble. Their last night out was at Ramble Falls. How great the Creator!

"Home at last," Raymond said. "Even though we had a great time, there's no place like home." Maria agreed with him. They fixed a snack and some iced tea. Raymond went to the shower, while Maria called Jody. She told him all about their trip, and said they would do it again when he and Allison could go with them. She then called her parents. They were so glad that she was back home. When Maria finished telling her Mom all about Gatlinburg, and the Aquarium, Jo said that she and Paps would surely take that trip. Paps was very happy for Maria and Raymond. "You could not have found a better man. At least, that's my opinion." Maria said she agree with him a hundred percent. Jo wanted to know if Maria and Raymond had time to drop by before bed time. Maria said No, that Raymond was in the shower, and she was headed in that direction, and then to bed.

Daybreak came early. Maria couldn't believe it was time to get up. Raymond pulled her toes. "Are you going to fix breakfast, or am I?" Maria rolled over and whispered, "I guess you are. I'm not up yet." Raymond left the room, and went to the kitchen. Maria got her feet on the floor, and got dressed. When she got to the kitchen, Raymond was making toast. "Is this all we're having?" she inquired."No, you have to scramble eggs." Maria moaned, "What a pitiful breakfast." Raymond said, "Looks good to me. I'm used to it." They were both almost late for work. They both felt that they had just gone to bed when the alarm went off. Raymond kissed her, and they both took off in different directions. Raymond's friends were so glad to have him back. Some of their decisions were a bit heavy. "Now, you're the boss, so take over." Maria was equally greeted by her friends.

Both Raymond and Maria were given gifts to take home. Both were surprised that each of them had a load of wedding gifts. Maria's mind went into a spin as she tried to imagine what was in each package. They decided to wait until just before bed time to open the presents.

Paps and Jo came to witness what was in the gift boxes. Raymond was not at all excited. Maria was too excited to open the packages. Jo helped her. She wanted Raymond to go first. He had three, and began to tare off paper. He had an electric drill, a C.D. player with a couple of CD's, and a tool box full of tools. He was now excited. He had said he would build himself a shop in the back yard. He loved making different things from various woods. Maria began her task. She had more paper to tare off then Raymond did. Her spirits were too elevated. Her first exposed gift was a nice size slow cooker that she had been wanting. She continued, and found a set of Christmas dishes, a set of satin sheets, a four slice toaster, and some sexy underwear. After all the trash had been cleared, Jo went to the kitchen to make some coffee to go with the cookies she had brought. Paps pulled some envelopes from his pocket, and handed them to Raymond and Maria. They were from the church. They were amazed to find gift cards to several stores at the mall, restaurants, and grocery stores. How great!

Maria got her films developed, and carried out her plan with Raymond and the black bear. She sent a picture to Allison, and to Jody. She carried one to work, and hung one on her wall. She was also planning to paint one on a large canvas. As Raymond entered the birthing center, the girls started laughing. "You sure outran that bear, didn't you"? He confirmed that he surely could outrun a bear, unless it was a mama bear who had lost her cub. As they ate lunch, they thanked the girls for their gifts. Raymond had the last word. "Whoever gave Maria that pretty underwear, thank you, thank you." Everyone laughed as they were going back on duty. He whispered to Maria, "I have never seen a more beautiful rump." She hit him.

Jo called Maria to say that she would pick her up for art class, and that Paps had a plan for him and Raymond. What a surprise! Paps had bought a golf club and balls for Raymond. And the two of them would play golf on art days, which was twice a week. Raymond showed some surprise as well as pleasure. He finally said, "Thanks Paps. I've been thinking about this for quiet a while." Paps asked, "Then why didn't you ever get into it?" Raymond laughed, and said because he never knew which end of the club to hit the ball with. Paps slapped him on the shoulder, and promised, "Young man, you're fixing to learn." Paps then handed Raymond another envelope. Raymond opened it. In total shock, he pulled out a one year membership card to the City Golf Club.

Maria felt free now that Raymond would be busy the same evenings she painted. She began, at home, painting Raymond and the black bear. Jo was home-painting a picture of Jody all dressed up at his Mom's wedding. Jo said that picture was of the best looking man she, or anyone else, had ever seen. Maria agreed with her. "He gets his good looks from his mother," she said. Jo agreed with her. Presently, in class, she was painting a scenic view with a river running through it. Jo's main interest was painting old houses, and she had painted two that she was very pleased with. Jo always showed gratitude that Maria got her into painting. Jo was hysteric as she kept looking at Maria's painting of Raymond and the black bear. "How long will it take you to finish?" She asked. "Maybe three months, maybe six," was Maria's response.

That night Raymond talked about building his shop. The men would help him, but he had some decisions to make first. Where, how big, interior, and why-He wasn't sure right now. He did, at one time, have a shop back of his house. That was a long time ago, before his wife died and he sold their house. He enjoyed building tables, of any shape or size, book cases, or desks. Anything made from various kinds of wood was his pleasure. Then deciding just what finish he's put on each project, and doing it, delighted his spirits. Maria had a large back yard, and he could build whatever he wanted in it. She assured him that it was as much his yard as it was hers. If he didn't feel comfortable, then perhaps they should buy a home for themselves. Raymond had considered that, but was amazed that she said that.

Maria had a friend whose husband was a realtor. She talked with her about the idea of buying a house. The realtor came to the hospital and talked with her. What kind of house did she want? Where did she want it? How much did she want to put into it? Some of the questions, she had no answer for. She made arrangements for him to meet, at lunch one day, with Raymond. She told her parents, and they were expecting that to happen eventually. At almost the same time, thy both pleaded to pay for half of the house they would buy. Where ever it was, or how much it was, would not matter. Maria was not prepared for that. She was amazed at such a gift from them. She was also amazed that they could do that. Their financial value must be much greater than she imagined. Where did it come from? She knew they had money, but that much?

Raymond kept the appointment Maria had set up for him with the realtor. Maria and the girls went back on duty, while the two men discussed the pending business. The realtor, Marvin, took Raymond through a few neighborhoods and carried him through a few houses. Raymond would have to talk with his wife before a decision could be made. Maria told Raymond that night about her parent's offer. "No way." He said. "I'll take care of this myself." That really surprised her. In shock, she remarked, "I didn't know you had the means to buy a new house right now, with college expenses being what they are." He took her into his arms, and whispered, "Well, we never really talked about my finances, nor yours either. I know that Paps bought the houses, and paying college expenses for Jody too. That surprised me." She explained that her parents had sold a 500 acre farm with two houses on it, and a small farm with two houses on it, not to mention, four mules, tractors, and other valuables, before they moved. Raymond was now more surprised.

They sat down, and Raymond began to unwind. His parents had both been killed in an accident that was not their fault. His Dad was driving when a huge truck, owned by a beer company, ran a stop sign and smashed his Dad's car killing both of his parents. Being their only child, he was granted the settlement, which was quiet large. He was also the only heir to their home, and beneficiary to their insurance. He had always felt a bit sad using what had belonged to them, but now felt more free to do so. After all, that was their intent. He had tears dripping off his chin. Maria sat in his lap and embraced him. She had not heard that story before, and she had never asked personal questions. She had often wondered about his parents, but since he never spoke of them, she never asked about them. She sympathized with him, and wanted to do something to pull him out of the ditch he had fallen into. She kept rubbing his hand and kissing his face. She silently thanked God for her parents. Poor Raymond, she thought, He lost his wife right after loosing his parents. "Is there anything I can do to make you feel better?" She asked. Raymond came alive and said, "What you're doing feels good to me. Would you like to go to bed for a while?" Maria jumped up and pulled him up. Off they went.

Marvin, the realtor, met with Raymond and Maria after work and showed Maria the houses. A decision was not made that day. Raymond, teasing his wife, remarked, "I thought you would want a more elite neighborhood, and a much larger house." She hit him, and said, "The final decision will be yours. I don't have time to be burdened with it." Still teasing her he asked, "Suppose I buy a house that has no bathroom?" She snickered, "I don't think you could find one, but if you can live in it, I can." Raymond's response was, "There are so many reasons why I love you. I could never name them all. I have never been happier in my life, than I am right now. You are so loving, caring, and a positive thinker. You never moan or groan about anything. You're giving me a life like I never had." Maria replied. "That works two ways. I've never really been happy until I snatched you up."

All the girls were curious the next morning. "Did you find a house?" They wanted to know. One of the nurses had a hose for sale. She was on the threshold of bankruptcy, and wanted to sell before foreclosure. She talked with Maria on a secret basis. She had not mentioned it to anyone else. At noon, she carried Maria to her house. Maria was impressed as they pulled into the driveway. They strolled through the house with walk-in closets in all three bedrooms, and two and a half baths. The master bedroom's bath had a large walk-in shower. Raymond would love that. It also had double sinks for his and hers counter space. In the massive back yard was a storage building and a shop, Maria couldn't believe that. But there it was. What she liked most, was a living room and also a large family room. There was a large storage room off from the kitchen. That would be her painting room, she decided. She told her friend that Raymond would have to take the tour. That afternoon, she and Raymond went to see the house. Raymond walked around the house to the buildings in the back. "We'll take it," he said. "But you haven't seen the house yet." Maria warned him. "You make the inside decision, and I'll make the outside." He told her. Maria's friend thought that was funny and strange. They all met at the mortgage company the next day, and Raymond bought the property.

Chapter 10

Since it would be two weeks before they could move in, Raymond and
Maria planned to spend the week end at the lake house. Raymond
invited Paps and Jo to go with them. They graciously accepted his
offer. Jo had thought it was about time. They were both impressed,
and Paps said he'd like to have a lake house. Raymond took them for
a sail all over the lake. He anchored the boat at his favorite spot, and
they spent some time fishing. Maria and Raymond sang together from
time to time. Jo and Paps appreciated that. Jo screamed, everyone else
jumped, and Paps went to her. She had caught one quiet large catfish.
"That's a nice size fish, why did you scream? I thought you had caught
an alligator." Paps said. They all laughed, except Jo. Raymond said "Let's
keep fishing. Maybe Mom didn't scare the rest of the fish away." It was
Maria's turn, another catfish. Paps pulled in a fair size mullet, and the
four of them caught eleven fish. They all took a roll in preparing dinner.
The men cleaned and fried the fish. The women had already made cold
slaw. Jo fried the corn bread. All this was not quiet what Raymond
called hush-puppies, but it was good. They sat on the front porch and
chatted until bed time. "Are we going out again in the morning"? Paps
asked. Raymond said, "Yes, if you want to." Paps winked at Raymond
and said,
"Then we'll go."

The women didn't go out on the boat that morning. They spent some valuable time together. Jo wanted to wander through the cabin, then they went outdoors and rambled around. Finally they went out on the dock just looking around and talking. Jo, in a surprise, said "What are they doing?" Maria didn't have a clue what she was talking about. She looked up and down the lake wondering, when Jo pointed her finger to a dock about two doors down. What are they doing there? She thought. Maria saw Raymond and Paps walking around. Now, she was wondering what they were doing. The men returned, and Maria asked, "No fish?" Raymond told her they had not been fishing. They had just been browsing around looking the place over. Paps hadn't been on a searching cruse of the lake. They all went into the cabin, and the women fixed cold drinks. As they sat there talking about the lake, Paps said to Jo. "We found a cabin for sale about two doors down. I jotted down the information, and think I'll call about it. Wouldn't you like for us to have a lake house?" Now, Jo and Marie knew what they had been up to. Jo responded, "You know I would." Two weeks later, Paps was owner of the cabin.

While Paps and Jo were busy getting some furniture moved into the cabin, having new furniture moved into the house, and doing some updating on the dock, they took enough time off to buy a boat. Raymond and Maria hired movers to move them into their new house. As soon as they moved in, Raymond began doing some work on the shop. He replaced shelves, and put in cabinets and tables. The shop was already well wired. He painted the interior and put in two windows. Maria was pleased that he had brought a few pieces of his own furniture. The rest of his things, he moved into the storage shed. His house was now empty. His plan was to rent it. Maria loved her new home. It was more spacious than the one she had. She too, would rent the other house. Jo and Paps came and helped her to get everything in place. It took a few days for her to know where everything was, especially her kitchen items and linens. Jo too, was moving her old furniture to the cabin, and placing some new in her house. It was time for the kids to come home. They knew about the moves, and were anxious to witness the changes.

As Jody and Allison drove into the circler driveway, Maria and Raymond were standing there to greet them. Both of the kids were astonished at the sight of the new house. They were anxious to take the inside tour. "Show me my room first."Allison asked. "No, mine first." Jody argued. Maria led Jody and Raymond led Allison. They were each well pleased, but there was a shadow of doubt if they would ever come home again. There would, of course, always be visitations, but never on a permanent basis. Allison told Maria about her boy friend, and wanted permission to bring him with her on her next visit. Maria assured her there would be no problem with that. They put a single bed in Jody's room for the boy friend to sleep in. Raymond approved. Jody then surprised them by saying that he had a girl friend, but she wouldn't be coming home with him anytime soon. Maria asked, "Any why have we not heard about this before?" Jody laughed at her, and said, "Until recently, she has just been a friend, but that has lately changed. By the way Mom, are we going to eat tonight?" Maria said they should, why not he and Allison go to the kitchen and fix something. Allison replied, "No, no, we don't even know where the pots and pans are." Raymond said, "You lazy bones. I'll fix something." He went into the kitchen and fried some fish and corn bread. There was a bowl of slaw in the refrigerator. They were greatly impressed when Raymond called them to the table.

Allison noticed the 10x12 picture of her dad running from a black bear. She loved the one Maria had sent her. She wanted to see the painting Maria was doing. Maria had kept it hid from Raymond until she had finished it. She took Allison and Jody into her art room, and showed them the painting. They were each mesmerized. Neither of them knew that Maria had accomplished so much. Jody said the only thing wrong that he could see was whether Raymond was running from a black bear or a black bull. Both Maria and Allison knocked him in the head. Maria pointed out to him that black bears didn't have horns. Jody said all bulls didn't either. Allison asked Maria, "Do you want me to hit him again?" As they left the room, they found Raymond cleaning up the kitchen.

They talked about the college events and learned that Jody was actually preaching at his church once a month. His girl friend attended the same church, and played the piano on a regular basis. She was from the Atlanta area, and Jody had met her parents. In fact, he had spent the week end at their home twice. They were Christians and active in the same church he attended. Allison had visited her boy friends parents a few times, but never over night. They too were Christians and she like them. Raymond commented, "I'm glad you both have met someone special, but keep in mind you've got another year to go, at least." Maria asked Jody if he was going for a higher degree. He said he'd surely get the Masters. Paps wanted him to go for the Doctorate, and he may some day, but not now. Allison would also go for the Masters.

After church Sunday morning, the entire family went to the grandparent's lake house. They made sandwiches and tea, and everyone ate before Allison and Jody had to leave. Paps had a private talk with Jody, as he usually did. He told him that the lake house and the boat now belonged to him. Paps had bought it in Jody's name. Jody was not prepared for that. He asked Paps, "Why Paps?" Paps replied, "Because you are all we have. I pray you will outlive me and your granny. I trust you to let us claim it, as long as we live, or able to enjoy it, He also told Jody that both the houses were in his name. He told him where the paper work was kept. He said Maria also knew where the paper work was kept, but she did not yet know that the cabin and boat were already in his name. Jody let Allison drive back to Atlanta. His mind was in a spin.

Maria didn't tell her parents about Jody's girl friend, but she couldn't get it off her mind. She was very glad that he had met a girl he liked, or loved. She kept reminiscing that he was not a kid anymore, no matter what she and Raymond thought. Maria and Raymond talked that night. They were both well pleased at the progress their children were making. Allison would surely make a fine teacher, but neither of them could, yet, see Jody as a preacher. They were most grateful for the experience he was getting from his church. Neither of them, at that time, could imagine Jody standing behind a pulpit. Raymond suggested, "Let's drive over there one week and attend his church. Better yet, let's find out what week end he will be preaching and go then." Maria agreed, but wondered if their presents would make Joy a bit too nervous to properly perform his duty. Jody looked almost like Paps, she imagined. How glad she was. Jo had thought too that Jody looked much like his grand daddy. Maria mentioned that to Raymond. "He looks a lot more like Paps than he does his Mom or Granny." He said.

Monday morning came early, for the two who over slept, and forgot to set their clock. If Raymond was late, it wouldn't matter. Someone else had the keys. Maria phoned the hospital to say she was not feeling well, and would like to have the day off. Her wishes were granted. Raymond went on to work, and Maria went to her art room-that Jody called her studio. She spent most of the day there dabbling in paint. She didn't feel the least bit sorry for taking the day off. She kept telling herself that she needed it. Now and then a woman needs some quiet time. This was her time. She had not experienced peace and quiet for a good while. She also did some house work. Everything was not yet in its place. She also did some work in the kitchen. She baked an apple pie, a ham, and made a couple of casseroles. Raymond loved those, and when they sat down to eat that night, he almost lost his breath when he saw all the food she had fixed. When they had finished eating, they went into the back yard.

There were a number of things that needed Raymond's attention. The shop needed a few more tools. The storage shed was full of his furniture and lots of stuff. The shed obviously was not leaking, so it was alright for now. He took a day off and made more cabinet space, and built a center table that he could walk around while working with the sander and saws. He bought some paint and put a new look in the interior of the shop. Then he went shopping for variety of boards. His first project was to build a large desk for Maria, one large enough to hold her canvas, paint, brushes, and paint books. He would not tell her until it was finished. That would be her birthday gift. She needed a book shelf, since her books were scattered all over the house. He would some time later build a desk for Jo. Right now, however, he had another load to free himself of. And, before he could build anything, he had to decide just how he would do it. The book shelves in particular, had to fit the need. It was so obvious that Raymond's dream had come true. He had a wired workshop.

Paps dropped by. Raymond hadn't showed up for golf lately. In fact, he had missed four days. Paps wondered if anything was wrong. He found out when he got into the shop. Jo was in the house with Maria trying to tell her some things that she should or shouldn't do. She wanted to know if Jody and Allison would ever get married. In shock, Maria finally decided it was time to tell her. "No. Allison is dating some one else, and will probably be engaged to him soon." Jo almost couldn't handle that. "Why did she and Jody break up?" Maria explained that Jody and Allison were never together. She also told Jo that Jody had a girl friend too. "Is he about to get married? I hope he will finish college first. Where will they live?" Maria wiped her face and told Jo that Jody was not engaged and certainly not getting married any time soon. She said she didn't know where he would live after his education was completed. That would depend on where he would find a job. "Mom, let's get something to drink and go on the porch. I need a break. "Where is Paps this morning?" Jo answered, "He's in the back yard with Raymond."

Allison came home that week end and brought Wallace, her boy friend. She had called and expressed a desire to bring him. There was something she wanted to talk with her Dad about. Maria and Raymond had guessed the truth, she was engaged. It was time for them to meet Wallace, and they had told Allison that he was welcome to come with her. He was a very friendly young man, and was also preparing to become a math teacher. Immediately Raymond noticed the ring on Allison's finger. Raymond began thinking where would they live, would his only child ever come home again. Atlanta was a bit too far for her to stay. When he had grand children, they would surely need to be near him. Maria fixed a good dinner, and the four of them sat down together while they ate and chatted. Maria and Raymond had already pledged not to ask and personal questions. They didn't have to, Wallace and Allison talked and shared things with them. At church the next morning Allison introduced Wallace to Jo and Paps, the pastor and his wife, and her friends. After the services ended, the engaged couple left.

At work the next morning, Maria told the good news. "Is that girl old enough to get married?" some of the girls asked. Maria was about to say no, but then recalled that Allison was almost twenty two. She was on the finish line of her last year of college, since she was not planning for a Masters degree at the present. She would not be married before graduation in September. She would teach at high school level. A bell rang calling Maria and others to the birthing center. Chat time was over. Maria loved being called to duty. She loved helping a woman to become a mother. Most of all, she loved that new born who had been struggling to see the world. Was there anything she loved more than helping to deliver babies? Well, yes, she loved more than anything else helping Raymond to cool his adredlin. The lullaby sounded loud and clear, but the baby did not make it. Maria came apart, lost control, and sobbed so loud that she had to be escorted out of the room. Dr. Lopez went to her, placed his hand on her shoulder, and said, "We can't save them all. But, we do save most. Don't think of the one lost, think of all those we saved." She wanted to tell him to kiss her foot, but she didn't.

That evening was paint classes, and Maria was sure anxious to get the brush in her hand. The colors of paint lifted her spirits, and she needed that. Jo sensed something was wrong with Maria, but asked no questions. She would find out later. They were painting birds flying over the ocean. And as usual, painting water and sky gave her a sense of peace and calm. Raymond picked her up from class, and took her out to eat. She talked about painting until they sat down to eat. Raymond became aware that Maria had a problem. He asked her what was wrong. Tears filled her eyes as she told him about the baby. Raymond almost cried with her. He said. "Accidents happen. Everyone is limited to what they can do. I know you did all that you could, and so did Dr. Lopez. For some unknown reason, it must have been God's will. The life the baby would have to live might not have been worth living. Everybody dies, even babies." Maria stared at him. He continued, "I came to that conclusion when I lost my parents. It was a terrible accident, but it might have been best for them. It was sudden, and they had no suffering. That baby will never know sorrow, heartache, want, nor pain." Maria nodded her head in approval.

Dr. Lopez called Maria the next morning and told her to take the day off. She was most surprised. After she told Raymond, he called his most worthy employee to tell him that he would be in charge for day. Raymond was also taking the day off. He told Maria to get ready for a day at the lake house. He said he felt like some boat riding. That lifted her spirits, and she knew that was his intent. Out in the boat, they talked and played. Raymond raced, turned sharp curves, dropped anchor, and even did some fishing. Maria caught a fish before he did. It was the largest trout either of them had ever seen. Raymond referred to Maria as his fishing partner. She was so excited. They ate lunch, put the fish on ice, and took the jet skeet out for a fun afternoon. They went home rather early and went to bed. After a good nap and needed rest, Raymond told Maria to get dressed for another trip. He wouldn't tell her where. She hesitated, but got dressed. He took her to their favorite barbeque restaurant. They went to bed early, and tomorrow would be a new day.

Chapter 11

Maria went by the V.A. hospital to see Paps. She knew he worked in the Emergency Room, but she had not been there. It was easy to find, and he was very glad she had dropped by. He was on duty, but not busy at the time. She sensed that he was not feeling too well. She asked if anything was wrong. He responded that he had a slight cold, but nothing to complain about. Maria laughed and asked if he had taken an aspirin. He patted her on the back and assured her that she was not the only doctor in the family. She went on to work, but couldn't get her mind off Paps. Her friends wanted to know about her day off. She told them all about her and Raymond's fun, then promised to take them to the lake on a Sunday afternoon when most of them were off duty. She promised to do it very soon.

One of the girls told Maria that Raymond had just walked in. She met him outside her door. Her heart was pounding. Why was he here at this time of day? She rushed to him. "What is it?" she immediately asked. "It's Paps. He's had a heart attack and is presently in the E.R. Your Mom is with him. She called me." Raymond and Maria immediately left to go be with Jo. Jo told them it was a mild attack, and that he would be alright, for now, at least. As soon as they were allowed to see him, Maria rushed into the I.C.U. Raymond was behind her with his arms around Jo. Maria was relieved when she became aware that her Mom was calm. She knows more about this, than I do, Maria thought. Paps was not speaking, because of medication, they were told. Only Jo was allowed to stay any longer in the I.C.U. Raymond and Maria went to the cafeteria for a snack and a break. Maria then went back to offer her Mom a break, which Jo refused. Raymond took lunch to Jo, and she was allowed to eat it in Pap's room. Paps woke up and told them all to go home. "Give me a break." He teased. He appeared to be doing fine, so the other three went home.

Maria couldn't decide if she should call Jody. Raymond suggested that she wait until tomorrow morning. They would know a little more about Pap's condition then. Maria agreed. As they were going to bed, the phone rang. Raymond beat Maria to it. Thank God, it was Jody and not the hospital, Raymond whispered to himself. Maria had no choice now, so she told Jody of the family tragedy. She explained to him there was nothing he could do, so don't come home now, wait until the week end. He promised. "What did he call for?" Raymond asked. "Just to talk, I guess." Maria replied. They both said a prayer for Paps and Jo, and then went back to bed. Maria couldn't sleep. If Paps survived this heart attack, there would be others, or at least one more. She began to worry about her Mom. At age sixty, her Mom would get through anything. She was always a strong woman, and this, no matter the final result, would not bring her down. Jo was a person who would live, laugh, and paint as long as she was breathing.

Paps came home a few days later. He appeared to be doing well, and said that he was. He was given a month off from work, but decided during that time that he would not go back. Death had knocked at his door, and he had other things to do before he opened it. He and Jo would go to the lake house for a few days or weeks, whatever they decided. He wanted to enjoy the rest of his life at the highest peak. He would sure do a lot of boat riding. He loved the boat. If he never caught another fish, that would be fine. It was the drifting on the water that he wanted most. Paps and Jo packed a few things and went on their vacation. They told Maria that they would be gone for about two weeks. She was a bit afraid and told her Mom. Jo said, "Let him do what he wants to do, while he can. If anything goes wrong, I have a phone in the cabin." Maria was thinking there was no phone in the boat, but said nothing. As they were leaving, Paps asked Raymond if they would come for the week end and bring Jody if he came home. Raymond said they would.

Jody did come home and couldn't believe his grandparents were not at home. He drove on home, and was much relieved when his Mom came running out to greet him. If there was anything wrong, she wouldn't be here. He immediately asked about his grandparents. Maria told him and comforted him by saying that she and Raymond, and of course, Jody were going to the lake in the evening. Jody was pleased; He needed a week end vacation too. As soon as they had a snack, Raymond was ready to leave. He had come home early, to get an early start. He and Jody embraced each other, and Raymond assured Jody that he would keep watch over Paps and Jo. "We'll stay until Sunday night, then go back about Wednesday afternoon. Every two or three days, we'll check on them." Raymond assured Jody, "We'll leave Sunday morning and go to church, then go back to the lake, and I can leave from there." Jody said. Maria was so proud of her son. He was not going to miss a day at church. Why should he? She wondered if Jody would be strong enough to preach Pap's funeral, if it became necessary.

Maria called her Mom before she went to work. Jo said they had a great time with the family over the week end. She was so glad they had come. She told Maria that Paps had talked about Jody ever since they left. They were not going out on the boat today, but would hang out around the dock, and screen porch. Maria told her Mom that she and Raymond would see them again about Wednesday. She confirmed that Jo had her work number. Raymond stayed near his phone at work. Hr also told his employees to watch out for a phone call in case he had to be out for some reason. Pastor Harris called. He said that Jody had put both of his grandparents on the prayer list. The church would take some food over as soon as they got back home. He also mentioned that Jody would be back on the week end. He didn't tell Maria that, but it didn't surprise her. On Wednesday, Paps was doing good. He was talking normal, and eating well. His only symptom was being weaker than usual. Instead of staying two weeks at the lake, they made it one.

Jody obtained permission to bring his girlfriend home for the week end. Maria was most anxious to meet her. Jody had talked more about her on his last visit. Tammie was a tall, slim girl, which made her and Jody look good together. She was only a year younger than Jody. They had met in class over a year ago. She was getting her degree in English Education, and desired to become a high school teacher. She was also studying music and would, in some way, get involved in it. Tammie was very friendly and appeared to be a good match for Jody. They seemed to like many of the same things, and were real good in conversation with each other. She would be going to church with them Sunday, and would be playing the piano. How did she know? Because Jody had made arrangements with Pastor Harris before he came home. Maria and Raymond decided that Tammie was the best piano player they'd ever had. Paps and Jo agreed, and of course, so did Jody. Raymond and Tammie sang one hymn together, and everyone applauded. Maria told Jody that Tammie was welcome to come anytime she wanted to. "Mom, this may get more serious than you are thinking." Jody told her. Maria kissed him good bye and said. "It's your choice."

Marie and Raymond both had a head full of rolling stones. What if this, and what if that, kept rambling through their thoughts. Would both Jody and Allison come back home to live, would they stay where they are, or would Jody follow Tammie and Allison follow Wallace. Raymond said, "We'll probably be grandparents in a year." Maria told him to shut up. She began thinking about her Dad. Why did he leave the hospital and go to the lake? Yes, he was home now, but he was too smart to have made such a foolish decision. "Let's go see about Dad." She and Raymond got into the truck and left. Her parents were watching a movie on television. Maria and Raymond joined them. Maria noticed tears in her Mom's eyes-maybe the movie, she thought, but it was not a sad movie. Maria wanted to ask her Mom what was wrong, but didn't. After the movie ended, Jo went to the kitchen and Maria followed her. "Is there anything wrong?" Maria asked. "Not right now, but surely later. He's too weak." Maria hugged her Mom and said, "You know recovery takes time."

"Let's do something different." Raymond suggested. "Like what?" Maria asked. "Let's go down to the river park and stroll through it. We seldom go to the old down town. That river walk is fascinating. There are tables and benches where one can sit down and look over the river. The Savannah River is wide and offers several areas of interest." Maria wasn't too interested, but agreed. She had strolled up and down the River Walk, and yes, it was a good place to ramble around. They had even been to the one in Savannah, but the one here in Augusta was more fascinating. She put on a pair of jeans, and sandals, and told Raymond she was ready. At the park, they bought a box lunch and ate on the river. Maria decided that was actually the best relief she'd had in several days. She was too interested in her present territory to worry about Paps; they walked around the original down town and discovered a few restaurants that they would try at another time. The meandering around was a needed relaxation for both of them.

"Call Jody," Raymond said. "And tell him we will be there Friday night." Maria almost hesitated, but didn't. "I'll call Allison." Raymond added. The calls were made and the visit was wanted. Both Jody and Allison were glad their parents were finally coming. Maria told Jody to make arrangements for them to see Tammie if possible. Jody would make motel reservations near the campus. He asked if they could go to church with him Sunday, and the answer was, "Of course, that's one of the main reasons we're going. Jody called his minister and told him the news. Arrangements were made for Jody to take over the sermon. Even the minister wanted to impress Jody's parents. Tammie wanted her parents to meet Raymond and Maria. Dinner arrangements were make for Sunday after services. Wallace and his parents wanted to meet them, and would also meet them for lunch. "I just hope we can handle the guest at lunch. How many? Maybe ten or more?" Raymond asked. "At least that many." Maria added.

Maria didn't see anyone during the sermon except Jody, standing so straight, speaking so great, and so handsome like his grandfather. She smiled at him during the entire sermon, otherwise she might have cried. Raymond kept squeezing her hand. Tammie played the piano. She and Jody sang one hymn together, during which time both of them kept their focus on Maria and Raymond. After the sermon ended and the last "A Men" was said, Jody held up his hand and said "Just a minute. Don't forget that God forgives all who ask, but not those who don't ask. If you want to stay on the road home, don't forget to ask." Introductions were made. They talked briefly, were greeted by the minister, and then went to lunch. They were seated in a private room. The ten were there, plus the minister and his wife. Everyone appeared relaxed and enjoying the meal and friendship. Wallace's Dad sat next to Raymond and they enjoyed their chat. Maria sat next to Tammie's mother, and each of them expressed their appreciation for each other's child. After they had finished eating, Maria and Raymond were invited by Tammie's parents to go home with them for a while. There they each became friends as they relaxed and spoke of their children.

Raymond and Maria left early to get home before dark. She had to check on her parents. Raymond was a bit too quiet, Maria thought. "We sure had a great visit, didn't we?" she asked. Raymond immediately responded. "Yes, we had a great visit and heard the best sermon ever. I almost couldn't handle the way he ended it. I thought he did excellent, and I told him. Maria patted his knee. "Thank you. I told him to come home when his work is finished at the college. Maybe he could find a job there, and we could hear him every week." They spoke of Tammie. It sure seemed to be a serious link between her and Jody, though neither of them mentioned it. Raymond said they would soon. He told Maria that Allison and Wallace would be getting married sometimes during the summer. Allison would not be coming home. She and Wallace had already been accepted in a teaching position at two different schools, but not far apart. Wallace's parents were looking for a house near the schools for them. Raymond said that he told Allison that she had a hose waiting for her here in Augusta. He told her she could sell it to help pay for another one if she chose to do so. Jody already knew that he had a house in Augusta waiting for him. But right now he didn't know just where he would land. He was already searching for a position. "He will not come home." Raymond remarked. "Shut up!" Maria said.

Paps and Jo were doing fine. He had no problem except for weakness, and each day he felt a little stronger. Jo had gotten back in her art classes and they had done a little yard work. They planned for a small garden of vegetables that could be eaten raw. They were both strong believers in raw vegetables and fruits. The idea gripped Raymond and he, after talking with Paps, decided to plant a small garden in his back yard. He, too, liked raw vegetables, but never given any thought to having a garden. Raymond found out from Paps what tools and equipment he would need, and, in case he would gorger, he made a list of what seeds and plants to buy. "I'm learning late, but a lot from your Dad. He told Maria.

Raymond never thought he'd become a farmer, but with Paps pushing him in that direction, it really wasn't much of a task. Paps gave instructions, Raymond followed. He, not only had his own garden to do, but most of Paps'. After the soil was tilled and fertilized, gardening became a pleasurable piece of work. What Raymond liked most was picking out just the right seed and plants. Maria wanted lots of tomatoes. Her Mom had always canned tomatoes, and they would eat them in soups, stews, as a gravy over rice, plus many more uses. She also wanted green onions and squash. She got her wishes. Raymond and Paps got a great idea. Bring the women out to help put out the plants. It didn't take near as long to get the work done, having four laborers instead of two. Raymond really got carried away. He now decided to plant some pecan trees, peach trees, and blooming shrubbery. Maria asked, "Are you planning to retire and just do yard work?" Raymond said, "No, but you might have to." She laughed. "Remember, the woman's work is inside, and the man's work is outside."Raymond said he did not know that. He added, "Then I'll pick the tomatoes and toss them on the kitchen floor, from there, they're yours, right?"

Jo and Paps were busy in their garden. At least, they had more time to do the work. Jo brought Maria about four dozen quart jars to can her tomatoes in. She would teach her how to make pickles and relishes. If Raymond's fig tree produced, they would make preserves. Raymond was amazed at how fast the garden grew. They were gathering vegetables in a few month, and Maria was canning tomatoes. She filled all of her jars. By the time the season ended, so had Raymond. Paps had not told him of all the work that had to be done after the seed were in the ground. Someone had to keep the weeds and grass out. "Never again." He said to himself.

Maria shared her garden with her friends. She made several meals of various tossed salads. Too many, Raymond concluded. She gave to Jody large bags of garden items to take to Tammie's mother. She enjoyed the thank you cards that she received. Maria looked forward to next year when they would do it again.

Chapter 12

Their most exciting trip they ever gook was to Jody's graduation. The four of them went together. Maria was so happy that her parents were with them. Jody was most pleased that all four had been able to come. He had feared, after Paps' health problems, that there would be only three to come. He thanked God for his grandfather's presence. They were escorted to their seats in the auditorium, and sat nervously waiting for Jody to march out on the stage. The wait was short. As Jody was handed his degree, one side of Maria's face was laughing, the other side was crying. The men, they were calmly smiling. The applauds were quiet audible. They also witnessed Tammie getting her degree. They also got to see Allison receive her degree. Raymond embraced Allison and said, "I'm so sorry you're not going to return home." She kissed her Dad, and promised faithfully to see him on a regular basis. As soon as Maria turned Jody loose, Paps grabbed him, and Maria embraced Allison. Wallace had gotten his degree about three months earlier, but he was there with them.

Jody didn't have a job yet, and planned to go home for a while. He was actually thinking about going for the Masters degree in the fall. He had not talked with anyone about this, except Paps. It was Paps' wish, and now Jody's. Allison would be home in a few days. She was with Wallace's family for a few days while his sisters were visiting. Also

Tammie would be there in a week or so to stay a few days. Raymond and Maria were so happy to have the kids back home for a while. Jody spent most of his time with Paps. Maria wondered about that. Something was going on between those two, maybe she'd find out one day. Jody finally told his parents that he would be going to Johnson City to get his Masters degree. Paps wanted him to do that. It wouldn't take him much over a year if he fit into that particular program. And, by then there may be a job available to him. That suited his parents. He was now calling Raymond his Dad and introduced him as such. Raymond felt good about that. Jody was certainly the only son he ever had.

The week flew by, Allison and Tammie arrived together, and, according to their luggage, they would be there for a while. For sleeping arrangements Raymond took the twin bed out of the storage house, and put it in Allison's room. Now they had a private bed. Maria managed a couple of days off from work. She and the girls had a great time together. They worked in the kitchen, straightened up the house, and got in some shopping. The girls appeared to have a great time on their visit. Raymond took all five of them to dinner one night to Jody's favorite barbeque restaurant. Wallace came. Raymond took another twin bed from storage and set it up in Jody's room.

Paps and Jo took the whole bunch to their favorite Italian restaurant. Jody did a great job entertaining everybody. He asked Maria, "Why do you never make spaghetti and meat balls that taste like this." She told him she couldn't because she was not Italian. The girls laughed. Wallace said to Maria, "You seem to really enjoy these girls. I know why too. Knowing that boy you've had to deal with." Maria bowed down to him.

Raymond took the day off, and they took all the kids to the lake. There, they really had fun. Raymond and Paps brought the boats out. Jody took Paps', and Wallace took Raymond's. The girls jumped in, and off they went. They were racing, and Paps didn't like that. Jody and Wallace sailed at high speed all over the lake. When they came back to the dock, Jody got the jet skis out. There is when the fun began. When they got back from that trip, everyone was soaking wet except Tammie. The rest had, in their foolish pranks, fallen into the lake. Paps felt like using a boat paddle on their butts, but the old folks kept quiet. Paps did get Jody off to himself. What he said to him, no one knows, but the boys did no more racing on the lake, even though, they took the boat out again after lunch. Maria and Jo had made potato salad and sandwiches. Jo made a gallon of tea. They all enjoyed their meal together. The kids were given two more hours before they would leave. Back to the lake, they went.

On the way home, they all talked at one time about the day. Each one thanked Maria and Raymond for their great fun visit. Wallace left following the girls. He promised to keep an eye on them. The next planned family trip would be to Wallace and Allison's wedding in about two weeks.

Maria and Raymond were a bit tired. As much as they enjoyed having the children home for a few days, peace and quiet was needed. Jody had gone to his grand parents for the night. He and Paps had things to do. Since both of his parents would be back on the job tomorrow, he'd spend that time with his grand parents. Jody needed a break too. He had worked hard the past year on unbelievable assignments. He loved doing research, but only if it had an ending. It seemed to him that most were endless. Yes, a few weeks off is what he needed. He and Paps had met Pastor Harris for lunch one day. They had some good conversations, and Jody learned the answer to a few questions he had. Pastor Harris appeared to be most pleased to have Jody home a while. He needed some help in the church office that Jody could take care of.

Allison called to announce that she and Wallace would be coming home for their wedding. That was a shocking surprise to Maria and Raymond. Their original plan had been to get married there where all her family lived. Maria pondered what happened to chance their plan. Shouldn't Allison given them a longer notice, and more information? Raymond had talked with Allison and merely related that they would be there the next week. "Are we suppose to make any plans or arrangements?" Maria asked. "Not that I know of," was his reply. Maria was quiet agitated, and was tempted to call Allison herself, but declined to do so. If Allison needed any help from her, she'd ask, after all Allison built her own trap, so let her walk into it.

Jody came home and it was obvious that he had a good time with Paps. He was acting normal again. "Mom, I know you are all jittery over Allison's new plans. I talked with her last night and she told me. They will be here Friday afternoon. They will be married at the church

Sunday, and they will be married by me." Raymond was also in the room. He made a choking noise. Maria placed both of her hands over her mouth, and made a terrible sound. Jody looked at them and asked, "What's wrong with you two? Don't you have a heart attack. Allison wants both of you sitting on the front row. So calm down. Raymond will walk to the alter with her, and after he has handed her over to Wallace, he will stand by her. Mom, you will stand by Dad. Wallace's parents will stand by him. When the wedding is complete, we'll all met in the fellowship room for a good meal together, including the wedding cake. From there the recently joined couple will depart to an unknown location for their honeymoon.

Maria said she had never felt more helpless. Raymond agreed with her. Why were they not more involved, what about Allison's dress, her bouquet, and who is furnishing the food? Surely the church would do that, but about the wedding cake? Where would they stay? Jody didn't know that. Jody talked with them again that night. Yes, the church would take care of the food. Jody was buying the cake. Pastor Harris was getting the word out to the church members. They were not to worry. Both Allison and Wallace were very smart, and certainly had the right to plan their own wedding. "They are not kids," Jody concluded. Maria felt much better, but Raymond didn't. He still felt that he should be more involved. Jody fixed the three of them a cheeseburger, and they began to calm down a bit.

Allison and Wallace came by Saturday night for a brief visit, and to drop her off for the night. Wallace went back to the motel where his parents and sisters were staying. Allison and Raymond talked briefly, but no mention was made about the plans. Sunday morning Wallace came by to pick up Allison. Jody rode with them to church. Wallace's family was right behind him. Raymond and Maria followed. Jo and Paps followed them. Maria smiled through the whole process. Allison was so beautiful. Wallace was smiling. Jody did a very nice wedding ceremony. After the groom kissed the bride, Jody embraced and kissed her on the cheek. During the reception, Maria and Raymond mangled with Wallace's parents. Maria introduced them to her parents. Maria and Raymond also reached out to Wallace's sisters. Wallace's father remarked. "I really appreciate the good ceremony Allison's brother did." That somewhat surprised Raymond, but pleased him. Jody had his camera and made several pictures of the bride and groom, and their families.

There were some gifts on the decorated tables there in the fellowship room. They did not open the gifts but loaded them into their car. Maria wanted to know what the gifts were. But, as Jody had reminded her, it was Allison's decision. Maria had given her satin sheets because she knew how Allison loved them. Jo had given kitchen utensils, Paps and Jo had given them a card containing two hundred dollars. What the church friends gave, no one had an idea. Maria noticed that both Allison and Wallace embraced Jody on their way out. Raymond saw it too, and whispered to Maria, "They are going to Lavona Island. Allison told me before she left. She'll call me in a few days. I gave her two hundred dollars."

Back home, Maria and Raymond tried to accept the facts, and head in another direction. Tomatoes got their attention. Jo had told Maria about canning tomatoes, and Maria was ready to take on the load. She and Raymond picked a bushel, and soon, the water was boiling. They pored the boiling water over the tomatoes, skinned them, cut them up into small pieces, put them in a pot to boil for seven minutes, then filled the jars, and screwed on the lids. Finished! Though Jo's instructions were short and easy, it actually took about three hours to get through the process. The next morning however, there sit over a dozen quarts of tomatoes. All Maria needed now was tomato recipes and Jo had many. Having stayed up late, they slept late, but both managed to get to work on time. Jody slept late. When he got up, his parents were both gone. Entering the kitchen, he saw what they had been doing. He ate and took off to help Raymond.

Maria shared her week end with the girls. They seemed to enjoy the wedding, even though none of them were there. When Raymond came for lunch, four or five of them ate together. One told Raymond that he would soon be a grand paw. That didn't hit him quiet right. Did she know something that he didn't? He wondered, but finally responded, "I don't think so." He glared at Maria. Surely, she would have told him if she knew anything. "Why would you think that?" he asked. They laughed. "Well, you know how a baby is created don't you? Too often newly weds don't give a thought to the facts. That causes men like you to become grand paws." Raymond caught on. He tapped her arm with his spoon, and said, "I am much too young for that."Maria laughed and agreed with him. I t occurred to her then what he had been thinking. At that time, Jody strolled in. He said to Raymond, "You didn't want me to have lunch? You just took off with out a word." That was funny to Raymond. "The truth is, I just forgot you were in the area. Sorry about that." The girls really laughed now. "This has got to be Jody." One said. Then Raymond introduced Jody as his and Maria's son. The girls knew. As they were returning to duty they said. "Come back and eat with us Jody, even if you do have to find your own way."

"How far is it to Johnson City?" Raymond wanted to know. Jody answered, "I don't really know, but I'll let you know when I get there. I know how to get there, and that's about it." Maria smirked, "I'm sure glad you know how to get there." "Mom, I'm not a first grader, I know how to read maps." Maria, acting surprised said, "That's right. You have already graduated from college. How time flies. I had forgotten." Jody turned to Raymond and remarked, "I'm really sorry you have to put up with you know who." Then Jody gave his Mom a big hug. "You know I love you, no matter what." She said she knew. He hugged Raymond, and said, "I love you too." His luggage was already in his truck, so he walked out of the room and got into the truck, and started on his way.

Maria and Raymond were both a bit nervous. Raymond had not heard from Allison, but he understood that a honeymoon was not the time to worry about phone calls. She would call in a day or two. Maria was concerned about Jody. She hoped he would like Johnson City and get his Masters Degree as soon as he thought he would. Raymond said, "I'm tired of strolling around the kitchen. Let's go down to the River Walk and stroll around, then pick up something to eat." That sounded good to Maria.

Again, Maria took her camera. They picked up a carry out meal, and sit looking over the river as they ate. They didn't talk about their children. They talked about things they could see from the park. They enjoyed the various reflections in the water, as well as the different kind of birds standing on the tree limbs. Before they left, they witnessed two alligators swimming toward them. After they had finished eating, Raymond pored them another drink. He was not ready to leave. By the time they took the walk back to the truck, it was getting late. Maria wanted to visit her parents before they went home.

Jo and Paps were watching a movie that was about to end. Their first question was, "Have you heard from Allison and Jody yet?" Raymond answered, "No, but we will as soon as they get around to it." Maria changed the subject. "We'll get back to painting next week Mom. I am ready" Jo then showed Maria a painting that she was doing at home. It was a basket of fruit, and would be a beautiful dinning room picture. "Are you about finished with your sea gulls?" Jo asked. Maria smiled and said she was almost finished. Maria then asked about her Dad. Jo said, as far as she knew, he was doing just fine. On the porch, the men talked about shop work. Paps was not too interested in it, but he did like to hear of the things Raymond was making. What he did not like at all was that the shop had robbed Raymond of his interest in golf, if indeed he ever had any. The women came out on the porch and Maria said to Raymond that it was time to go home. They got home relaxed and happy.

Chapter 13

While Maria and Raymond were eating breakfast the next morning, the phone rang. They both humped up. Maria picked up the phone. It was Jody. He had arrived safe and sound. He said that he not once got on the wrong road because his map was accurate, and he could follow it well. Maria replied, "Thank you for calling, Smarty." He laughed and said, "Bye." Maria sat back down and was telling Raymond what Jody had said. Raymond laughed and said, "I love his personality." The phone rang again, and Raymond took the call. I was Allison, and they were back home. She didn't offer many details. Raymond did ask her, "What do you mean home?" Her reply was, "Dad, you know." Totally relaxed, they both went to work.

It was a great day for Maria. Hearing the lullaby tune five times elated her ego. She helped the little ones make their arrival. She was filled with glee all day. After nine months of growing, they had finally become citizens. She shared the events of the day with Raymond. Then she went to tell her Mom. Of course, that was her job, but to help deliver five babies in as many hours was unusual. "Why don't you paint a picture of a birth?" Raymond asked her. Maria laughed, "And just where would I hang it?"

Raymond looked around. "I think the bath room would be a good place." Raymond had some good news too. "We did twice as much business today than usual. For some unknown reason, people were coming and going all day. At one time I thought I'd have to call Paps to come help us. He told Maria that the business was really growing, and he might have to hire more help. That was good news for both of them.

Raymond decided to close his business on Saturdays, now that Maria was also off on that day. Saturday was not a good day for him anyway. Now he could get some work done in his shop. He was close to finish on Maria's desk and table. He wanted to get that over with, so he could start on Jo's. Then he was going to make an old fashion shift robe for himself. He had too many things scattered around with no place to put them. He would make sure it matched the bed room furniture. Never before had he waited in such anxiety as he now did on Saturdays.

When he had finished the desk, he placed it in Maria's studio. When Maria saw the furniture, she couldn't believe Raymond had made it. Never had she seen any furniture that looked better. "Why don't you sell the business, retire, and go into furniture making. No one can do it better than you." Raymond remarked, "I'll do that someday. But to retire at forty five is out of the question. I'll wait about twenty more years. By that time, I could have enough money to open up my own furniture store." He kissed Maria, and said, "Thanks babe," Jo and Paps walked in during the excitement, and Maris showed them her new desk and table. Paps placed his arm around Raymond and said, "This is absolutely great work. And I'm not surprised that you did it. You can do anything you wish to do." Jo was as proud of Raymond as Paps was. Though she praised the work, she never mentioned wanting any for herself. Raymond had a surprise waiting for her.

Much to their surprise, Paps shared with them a well kept secret. He was going to add fifteen feet across the back of the other house. He knew the house now belonged to Jody, and he would, some day, need more space. The addition would only be three bedrooms and a bath. He explained that Jody would someday have a family of his own, and would need more space for children. "Who knows, he may become the father of ten." Raymond visualized the plan, and was most excited about it. Maria, in total shock, couldn't visualize anything. "Dad, the house already has three bedrooms and two baths." She said to Paps.

"I know that darling. Paps responded. "But they will have, besides children, parents, and grand parents, who may like to visit them from time to time. Jody will need office space. Maybe his wife will too. And a twelve by twelve foot play room would certainly be nice."Jo smiled at Maria and commented, "Let him do it. He's been talking about it for some time now."

Raymond told Maria to let Paps do whatever he wanted to do. After all, his time could be running out. She knew that, but didn't want him to over spend on something that was not needed. Paps had always taught Jody not to throw away his money. Now look what Paps, himself is doing. Was it that he just wanted to do something for Jody while he was still living? She listened to Raymond. "Paps only has one child, and one grand child. He wants to do something special for both of them. Doing this for Jody is a great gift to both of you. After all, you have a big house now, so let Jody have one." Maria was feeling a little better. "What if Jody never comes here to live?" she asked. Raymond told her, "That will be his problem. After he gets sixty five and retires, he will come here, if not before." She still didn't feel comfortable enough, but decided to let it go. She didn't need to add that to his worry list. Paps never said if Jody knew about his plan. Probably not, she decided. She asked Raymond what he thought. His response was, "We don't know. Jody surely knows a lot that we don't. He and Paps have certainly had enough private talks together. There is something about the lake property that we don't know. I think that property is already in Jody's name. There was something going on between them that Paps didn't want me in on. He didn't say so, but I sensed it and gave them their privacy." Maria exclaimed that she too sensed something about that. She said to Raymond that he was right. Jody wanted to tell her, but was probably under oath not to. She was certain that he wanted to share something with her, but couldn't.

Maria felt that she was in a broom sage being whipped by the wind. She couldn't get her brain to slow down, accept reality, and function normally. Then Dr. Lopez startled her. "Maria, follow me." He said as he ran past the table where she was sitting. She quickly obeyed. Now in the delivery room, she returned to her normal self. Triplets were born as naturally as any birth she'd ever witnessed. Here were three births in a row, and no complications. Triplets were rare, but so amazing. The surprise was awesome. The mother was overwhelmed. After that great accomplishment, Dr. Lopez said to the girls. "Let's go drink a coke and eat a candy bar. We deserve it. Cleaning up three is a job that calls for a break."

After noticing a silent vigil, with horror on her face, Dr. Lopez asked Maria, "Anything unusual going on in your world?" She didn't know what to say. "Yes, some very weird things. Some I can't comprehend, others I wish I couldn't." The girls laughed.

It's that husband of her's. He's up to something." Maria glared. "No, it's my parents. They are doing things behind my back. Nothing I would not approve of, but there are things buried in deep secret from me, that I feel I should know about." They asked what it was, and Maria told them about the add on to the house, and her thoughts on the lake property. Dr. Lopez suggested, "Thank God that your son is in the know." She felt better. Dr. Lopez got a call, and the short meeting ended.

When Maria got off duty, she headed to her parents. She would not ask any questions, but would open a path for them to fill with information. Raymond would be working late tonight, but would call her on his way home. Jo was alone in her painting room busy with her brushes. Paps was in bed taking a nap. Maria sat with her Mom and brought up varying subjects to discuss. Finally, Jo told her that Paps was not doing too well. He had been unusually weak for a couple of days, and was not eating well. He had given up golf after Raymond lost interest. Maria recalled, Paps was supposed to help Raymond with some shop work the night before, but didn't show up nor call. She shared that with Jo who knew nothing about it. Before Maria left, she went to check on her Dad. He was already asleep, but she awakened him. He mumbled a few words that she could not understand, but Jo told her to leave him alone, he was just weak. Maria obeyed.

Raymond called and Maria went home. Before she left, she said to Jo, "Mom, if anything happens you will call me won't you?" Jo said she would call her immediately. Maria asked, "Will you please call me before you call Jody? I can get here a little quicker than he can." Jo got the message. Maria shared her worry with Raymond. He knew something was wrong. Paps was suppose to go by his office to do some work, but didn't show. As Maria was making sandwiches for their late evening meal, the telephone rang. It was Jo,"Come now." She demanded. They heard sirens screaming a few blocks away. They ran, got into the car, and headed to her parents. When they arrived, Jo was standing behind the ambulance. They were taking Paps to the hospital. Maria wanted to know if he'd had a heart attack. Jo didn't know. Paps had simply asked to be taken to the E.R. He had shortness of breath and chest pains.

The three sat in the waiting room too long before they called Jo. She was the only one, at present, who could go into the room where Paps was. Yes, he had experienced another heart attack. He was not doing well. Some surgery was needed. As soon as Paps was placed into the Intensive Care Unit. Maria and Raymond were allowed to visit for a few minutes. Paps was not speaking. He barely opened his eyes a few times. Again, they waited and waited before Paps was taken to the operating room for by-pass surgery. When he was back in I.C.U, Jo was calm, but Maria was not. Jo talked with her. "There is nothing we can do, but pray and wait." Jo excused herself and secretly called Jody. She asked him not to come, but wanted him to know what was going on with Paps. Maria heard a P.A. mention heart murmur, but didn't understand it. She called Dr. Lopez who explained to her that it was the noise produced by blood flowing through the chambers and valves of the heart. She already knew Paps had hypertension, commonly known as high blood pressure, but she still didn't comprehend heart murmur. There was little she knew about the heart. Dr. Lopez showed up in the waiting room. Maria was surprised but pleased. Her curiosities were many. Perhaps he could answer some of her questions, if she could think of some to ask. The nagging questions remained within her. She said to Raymond, "I don't know what to do." Dr. Lopez, in trying to comfort her, said, "In times of confusion, as of now, perhaps the best thing is to do nothing at all. If you don't know what to do, usually, there's nothing you can do." That didn't relieve Maria very much, but she knew he was right.

A nurse came into the waiting room to tell Maria she could now see her Dad. Jo was very quiet. Paps was barely conscious, He glanced at Maria, but that was his only response. "How is he?" Maria asked her Mom. Jo was a bit too hesitant, "I really don't know, but we will soon." That was not the answer Maria seeking, but she realized her Mom was absolutely right. She went back to talk with Raymond. She was not going home until her Dad woke up and started talking. She would stand by her Mom. Raymond stayed in the waiting room the rest of the night.

In the early morning, Jo went to tell Raymond and Maria that Paps was awake. Raymond went home. Maria stayed.

Saturday morning, Jody showed up. A few hours later, Allison and Wallace drove into the driveway. Maria knew Jo had called Jody. What she didn't know, was that Raymond had called Allison. They all went to the hospital, and two at a time visited Paps. He was awake and more alert. He did admit that he was surprised to still be alive. Jody placed his arms around his Granny and took Paps' hand. He prayed for both of them. He prayed that God would bless them in whatever way would be best for them. Paps said, "Thank you Jody, I feel better already." Jody said, "You know I have been praying for both of you ever since Granny called me." They both nodded their head. Jo could not speak. Jody tightened his grip on her hand and proclaimed. "I really don't know what Mom and I would have done without the two of you. I do know Mom would have managed somehow, but life would not have been so good without you two." Jo wiped tears while Paps smiled. Jo left the room, and Allison came in. She embraced Paps and kissed his face. She embraced Jody, and said to Paps,"You know I love you, but I love my brother most." Paps said, "I'm so happy that Jody finally got a sister."

Jody took Allison and Wallace to church Sunday, but the others went back to the hospital. When the church services were over, the three went back to the hospital. Paps was felling somewhat better and had a stronger voice. Raymond took everyone to lunch in the cafeteria. They had valuable conversation. After lunch, Raymond and Maria went home to have more time with their children before they returned to their own destinations. Jody was well pleased with his new home, and greatly enjoyed his pursuit into the ministry. He was progressing well and was on schedule with his requirements. Allison and Wallace were both well pleased with their teaching positions. Raymond had a private talk with Allison and told her that she still had a house waiting for her, if she ever decided to come home. Allison told him that she and Wallace had discussed making a change. Raymond felt a sense of peace. Perhaps his daughter was actually coming home. He thanked God, went to bed, and slept all night. Jody left with the assurance that he'd be back for the weekend. Paps continued to improve and was able to go home. He and Jo were both surprised and pleased that he had pulled through the life threatening experience. It was difficult for Maria to return to work. Dr. Lopez gave her a week's vacation to be with her parents.

Maria went to her parents every morning and stayed all day. She didn't want to leave them in the evenings, but she needed to spend some time with Raymond. Jody came home the following weekend, as he had promised. This gave Maria a break because he spent much time with Jo and Paps. Jody took Raymond and Maria to church Sunday, and before they left, Jody and Pastor Harris had a talk that lasted a bit too long for Maria. What they were talking about, she wondered, but didn't ask. Jody left for Johnson City soon after they got home. Monday morning Maria couldn't decide if she should go back to work or stay with her parents another week. She didn't want to leave them, but listened to Raymond who told her, "It's time for you to get back on your own path. Your Mom can take care of your Dad, and she really doesn't need you to help her. If she needs you, she will call. It will be better for you to go back to work where you can talk and laugh with the girls." He pulled her close to him and patted her back. That's what she needed. She went back to work, but called Jo twice a day.

Raymond was right; she felt much better at work where she could talk and laugh. She thanked Dr. Lopez again for the week off. He told her"I've walked in your shoes. I was the main caretaker for my parents. If you need anymore time off, let me know." The girls had much compassion for her, and there was very little talking and laughing. What lifted her spirits the highest was the lullabies. At lunch some of her friends offered to help Jo whenever they could. Dr. Lopez, in an attempt to prepare her, told her to expect another heart attack not too far away. He told her that Paps' next attack would possibility be fatal. He patted her hand. "You need to be prepared, and you need to know that you can't prevent it. It happens. And I am sure that you already know that. So jump out of your denial attitude, and accept the results of reality. That's the best way to help your Mom." Maria was attempted to slap his face, but instead, she lay her head on his shoulder, and said, "Thank You."

Chapter 14

That night Raymond and Maria went to her parents and carried dinner. Maria let Jo put the food on the table and do the kitchen work. Maria stayed with Paps and tried to get into conversation with him. He was talking with a stronger voice, and smiled frequently. He said to Maria, "I want to share a secret with you. I'm not supposed to mention this, but you need to know." Raymond left the room and went to help Jo. Paps said in a low tone, "Pastor Harris is planning to retire before long. I'll hate to see him leave the pulpit, but I am somewhat excited about it too. He's been here a long time and is ready to leave." Maria asked, "Where is he going to preach now?" Paps answered, "Hr is retiring. As far as I know, he will still live here." She couldn't ask any more questions as Jo entered the room. The four of them ate and then sat and talked until time for Raymond and Maria to go home.

Maria shared Paps' secret with Raymond. They speculated on why the pastor was leaving, He was not old enough to retire. Who would replace him? Wouldn't they, as a congregation, vote on this, and shouldn't the church, as a whole, have this information? Raymond agreed with Maria. This should not be a secret. Maria would have asked Paps a few questions if Jo had not entered the room. Surely, Jo knew it, so why didn't they know the whole story? Maria wondered why her parents didn't share that with her before now. Why did they use a cover-up to conceal the truth from them? She would find out. She would ask Pastor Harris herself. Raymond told Maria that he would look into it Sunday. Jody came home Saturday as a surprise to his parents. Maria asked him if his Grandparents knew he was coming home. He said they did not know. Maria asked "Jody, is there anything going on that we should know about?" Jody said, "Yes, and you will know tomorrow. Please don't push it before then." He hugged his Mom. She glared at him, but kept her mouth shut. As thy entered the church, Paps and Jo were already there. That didn't feel right to Maria. They had not gone to church since Paps' heart attack. As everyone was seated, Pastor Harris stepped behind the pulpit and asked Jody if he would have the services today. Jody said he would and stepped up to the Pastor who went and took a seat with the congregation. Maria glanced at Paps, and he was wearing a smile from ear to ear. Of course, he knew Jody was coming home. Raymond held Marie's hand tight. She was nervous, confused, and a bit angry.

When Jody began his sermon, his parents began to settle down. They gave him their undivided attention. He was good to be so young. He had, however, read the Bible from cover to cover long before he got into Bible College, they recalled. Maria looked up at Raymond and noticed that he and Paps were wearing the same smile. Someone tapped Raymond on his back; he looked behind him, and there sat Allison and Wallace. When the sermon ended, Jody and Allison sang a hymn together. Then, Jody took a seat with her and Wallace. Pastor Harris took the stand and made a few announcements before he shocked the congregation speechless with the final announcement. He would be retiring in three months. He then added, "My replacement is entirely up to you, but I strongly recommend the preacher you just heard. Jody knows the Bible upside down and backwards. He is a very smart man, and would make you a great minister. Young ministers are more capable of bringing younger people into the church, and this church needs that." Everyone rose to their feet and applauded. Several voiced were heard, "Jody, Jody, Jody."

Raymond took the family out for lunch. Maria couldn't stop crying. Jo appeared as shocked as Maria was. Paps was a happy man. There, Maria summed it up, her Mom didn't know either. Jody confirmed her conclusion. Only Paps and the Pastor knew, and it was confidential.

Only the Pastor could reveal it. Maria never shared what Paps had told her. Allison and Wallace knew that Jody would be preaching and that's why they came. Jody had told her. After they had eaten they all went home with the Barfield's. Maria served ice cream, and they had a nice family time together. Then it was time for Jo and Paps to take their nap, and they left. Allison and Wallace soon departed. Maria turned to Jody. "Is there anything you need to talk with me about?" "Actually, there are a couple of things. Paps has added to my house, without my knowledge, and I want the interior painted. I want you to pick out the colors." The three went to see the house. It appeared to be finished, except for the painting. Jody told them if he got the job at the church, he wanted to move into the house. He hugged them bye, and left for Johnson City.

Raymond and Maria had much to discuss. They wanted to tell Jody that he didn't need that many rooms right now, and could move in with them, but didn't. They had already agreed to listen and offer no advice that was not asked for. They went to a paint store where Maria picked up some paint charts. She sat at her table and went through the colors. She liked all of them, but would Jody? She didn't have to match carpet since the house had hard wood floors. She finally chose grayish yellow, blue, and green to get the project started. Raymond knew someone who did interior painting, and hired him to do the job. Maria was calm and excited about redoing the house. She loved newly painted walls, and began looking at her own walls, but Raymond told her to forget it.

Raymond had finished Jo's desk and table. He called her and told her he was taking dinner to her house, and also a big surprise. When he and Maria arrived, Paps was sitting on the front porch, and Jo was standing in the drive way. A friend of Raymond's followed him to help unload the furniture. Maria carried the food into the house. "Mom, follow me." She said. "Who is that man behind Raymond's truck?" Jo asked. Maria told her, "He's a friend of Raymond's. Come on." Jo followed Maria into the kitchen. As they were about to call the men to come eat, Raymond stuck his head in the kitchen door, and said,"Mom, I need you for a moment." She followed him. "Tell me where to place this desk and table." Jo had both hands over her mouth. Maria and Paps entered the room just in time to see Jo with both arms around Raymond, Both Jo and Paps were very happy that Raymond had built the furniture. "I didn't know you could do this until I saw Maria's. You sure are a talented man. I love you Raymond." Raymond's helper left and the four sat down and ate lunch. Paps ate well, acted normal, and talked his usual self.

Maria told them about getting the house painted. Jo was as excited as Maria was. Jo said, "I almost fainted when the Pastor made his announcements. Why hadn't you told me?" Maria glanced at Paps, smiled and said, "I didn't know before you did. Jody told me later that he knew, but was under an oath of secrecy. "Well, tell him he almost disgruntled his Granny." Jo said. Paps said he felt sure Jody would be voted in for the pastor position. "The whole church knows him and his family, they have heard him sing and preach. I feel sure the position is his. And he wants it." So Paps and Jody had already the matter, Jo concluded. Maria knew too. She did understand, however, what secrecy meant. She prayed that Jody would get the job. He would come home again. Three months would give enough time to get his house in living condition. He would need a few pieces of furniture. Now that the painting was complete, would be the time to decide what he would need. She would talk to Jody about that. She still could not comprehend what Paps was thinking when he added so much to the house. The explanations he gave her, still didn't make sense.

Raymond told Maria that Allison was pregnant. He was thinking that she and Wallace would move into his house soon. He had talked with Allison about it, and she had expressed a desire to do so. She told Raymond that she and Wallace had inquired about local jobs, but hadn't applied for one yet. She would be able to finish out the year, and would then quit work to care for her child. At that time, they could use the rent free house. Maria was so pleased, she put on a record, turned the tune up, grabbed Raymond into her arms, and danced all over the room. He was as jubilant as she was. "So, the girls were right, you will soon be a grandpa." Raymond told her, "And you'll be a grandma." Raymond added, "Jody will get married soon, since he's out of school, then grand children will began jumping all over us." Maria Proclaimed, "I am not listening to you."

Maria had much to talk about at work Monday. She told the girls about Jody, the Pastor, and Allison. There were more questions than she could answer. They were more interested in Jody. That, too, was Maria's favorite subject. Jody would be home in about three months, and so many times Maria had wondered if he would ever come back home to live. She wanted Jody to find a local girlfriend. He had a couple of girlfriends at college, but nothing serious. Maybe now was the time. "There are some young girls working here at the hospital that are not married. Let's look around, maybe we could find him a local girl." One of them suggested. Maria thought that would be a good ides, but said "Let's wait a while and see." Another suggested, "Wouldn't it be amazing if he's already got a special lady that you don't know about?" The bell rang calling the girls back on duty. Maria was glad.

When Maria got home that evening, Raymond was already home. "We're going to a fish house tonight and then to the lake house." He told her. "What about Mom and Dad? I hate to leave them." Raymond smiled and said."I've already taken care of that. They're going with us. Here they are now." Maria greeted her parents, then said, "I have just got home, let me change clothes and I'll be ready." When she came back wearing shorts and sandals, Raymond whistled. They all stayed at Raymond's cabin. In the morning, Raymond took Paps for a short boat ride while the ladies fixed breakfast. After breakfast all of them went out on the boat. No one fished; they just meandered all over the lake looking and viewing everything in sight. They dropped anchor a few times to view new docks or anything unusual or different. Mostly they enjoyed the ride and the fish flouncing in the water. They were back in the cabin for lunch. Mom and Dad lay down for a rest.

Raymond and Marie went fishing near the dock. Raymond didn't have time to catch fish. He was too busy taking fish off Maria's hook. They were both having lots of fun. As soon as he got a fish off her hook, she caught another one. And so it went until Maria had caught sixteen fish, and Raymond caught four. After that, there were apparently no more fish in that particular area. They went back to the cabin. Mom and Paps were up, sitting on the screened in porch. They were watching Raymond and Maria, but couldn't see what was happening. They all had a big laugh when Raymond told them. Finally, Maria said to Raymond, "It's time for you to go clean the fish." Raymond replied, "You caught them, so you clean them." Mom and Dad thought that was funny. Maria said, "If I catch them, you clean them." Raymond said, "You clean your fish and I'll clean mine." Everyone was laughing. Maris said, "Raymond, haven't I told you the outside work is yours. The inside work is mind. So you clean the fish, and I'll cook them." Raymond said he had forgotten that. Mom and Dad were still laughing at them. The four had a great dinner together. The next morning they all went on another cruise over the lake, and then headed for home.

Maria was so grateful to Raymond for inviting her parents to go with them to the lake. They had not been out for a while. Paps didn't appear to get tired or weak. They both greatly enjoyed the trip. Raymond and Maria both enjoyed the fun her parents had. They deserved some pleasure time together. When they got home Maria and Raymond went in with the parents. Maria fixed some ham and cheese sandwiches. Jo poured the tea. Jo also had a banana pudding that they really enjoyed. "It's been forever since I've eaten banana pudding." Raymond said. Paps spoke up, "That's a shame. If your wife doesn't cook banana pudding, then what is she good far?" "To catch fish." Maria answered. Raymond winked at her. Then Jo announced," But you do eat three or four times a day. So give us women some credit, Mr. Barfield." Raymond bowed to Jo and said, "You are so right Madam." Jo hugged Raymond and said, "We do love you, our only son. And we thank you for such a wonderful day"

Jo called Maria, "Isn't it about time we got back in our art classes? Paps will go to work with Raymond, and that sets us free." Maria agreed. It had been a while since they had painted. "Yes, we need to go."When Raymond came home, Maria told him about her talk with Jo. He did not know that Paps would be with him, but said he'd call him to set up a time. The plan worked out, and the two women started a new painting. Maria needed that as well as Jo did. Working with colors elated her spirits, particularly if she was painting nature's backyard. That's what most of her paintings were. It came to her that she would need to hang some pictures in Jody's house before he moved in. The first one she thought of was the black bear chasing Raymond. Jody could call it a black bull if he chose to do so. It wouldn't matter to her. She had one painting of cabins on a lake; she would give that to Jody also.

Chapter 15

Jody called and asked if they would be interested in going to Johnson City for the weekend. He would be preaching at his local church. Of course they were interested, and began making plans. Maria's parents would do fine while she was gone. If they needed help, they could call Pastor Harris. Raymond called him and told him of his and Maria's plans. Pastor Harris told them to go on, he'd check on the parents. Maria felt a little guilty for leaving them, but Raymond assured her that they were in good hands, and the church knew how to get in touch with Jody. She picked her head up and they left. They arrived late, but Jody was anxiously waiting for them. "Did you stop and eat on your way here?" Jody asked. No, they did not, Raymond told him. Jody took their luggage and smirked, "Follow me." There in the front room sit a very beautiful young lady with long blond hair and blue eyes. Jody set the luggage on the floor, and said, "O, excuse me, you folks haven't met, have you? Linda, this is my parents Raymond and Maria Barfield. And this beauty is my finance, Linda Bradley. A wedding date hasn't been determined yet, but will be soon." Maria managed to faintly smile, but as usual in such surprise, she couldn't speak. Raymond went to Linda and hugged her. "Welcome to the family." He said to her. Maria stepped forward and took Linda into her arms. "I'm sure both of you are making a good choice," she whispered.

Jody announced that he and Linda were taking the parents to dinner. There was nothing on the menu that Maria wanted. She whispered to Raymond, "Order for me whatever you order for yourself." He did. She then turned to Jody, "I'm sure you know that we are too surprised, but then, you have always been full of them." She smiled. Jody pulled her finger and replied, "You are full of surprises too. I learned from you, remember?" Linda and Raymond were laughing at them. "I have one question. Do your grandparents know about your engagement?" Jody said, "Believe me, you are the first ones to know, except we two." Maria felt relieved. Now she knew something that her parents didn't. "Linda, are you in school?" Linda began, "No. I am in Real Estate with my Daddy. He is the broker at Atlas Real Estate, and I'm a realtor. I've been in the business for a couple of years. I really enjoy it. Helping people to find the right house for them brings me joy. I love helping others, and always have. It's a part of who I am." Both Raymond and Maria loved her already. She really impressed both of them. Maria said to her, "You have the most beautiful blue eyes I've ever seen. I'm sure they have a great influence in your abilities to help others. And your beautiful blonde hair is also an asset." She winked at Linda, and kept talking, "A beautiful blue-eyed blonde with a perfect smile, has great influence on others, especially good-looking young men like Jody." Linda smiled. "Thank you." She said. Jody was impressed. "I agree with you Mom." He said. By the time their food was served, everyone was relaxed.

Raymond said "As soon as you two have finalized your plans, call us. Do you know if you will be coming home or not?" Jody responded, "Definitely. That is, of course, if I get the pastors job. Linda said she was most excited about that. She was anxious for them to find out for sure. Raymond assured her that it was almost a closed deal. He said it was almost concealed at the first announcement. Jody agreed with him.

After Jody dropped his parents off at his apartment, he then took Linda home. Maria said to Raymond, "Why does one surprise after another keep slapping us in the face?" Raymond said, "Probably because we are human beings, and maybe our age has something to do with it." Maria slapped him on his shoulder. Jody came in, "Are you two fighting? I saw Mom hit you, in case you need a witness." Raymond told him, "Keep that in mind, just in case." Jody began telling them about he and Linda. They would be married at their local church, but if he got the pastor job, they would move into his house. Linda, he said, had no problem moving to Augusta. Her parents had no problem with her moving to another location. It wouldn't be too far for them to visit. If he didn't get the job, they would simply move to wherever he found a job. That didn't sound good to Maria.

Sunday morning, Jody took his parents to church. The pastor was out of town, and Jody took over. Linda sat with Maria and Raymond. She kept her eyes on Jody and wore a smile throughout the services. Maria was looking at Linda and Jody. Raymond kept his eyes on Jody. Then, another surprise, Jody and Linda sang a couple of hymns together. Maria knew, of course, that Jody was a singer, but how lucky for him that Linda was also a singer. So, that's how they got connected, Maria decided.

After the services, Linda brought her parents over to meet Jody's parents. They appeared to be very friendly, and invited them out to lunch. Jody joined them and introduced several friends to them. They all spoke highly of Jody. They had a friendly and pleasant lunch. Linda's parents expressed how pleased they were of their daughter's decision to marry Jody. They both spoke highly of him. Linda's mother said Jody was the one she would have chosen for Linda, if she'd had too. Jody thought that was funny. Maria was so pleased, and commented, "I think they both made a good choice. I am very pleased. Linda is the most beautiful girl I ever saw, and I'm sure she is as good as she looks." Raymond and Linda's Daddy conversed about their work and other things they were involved in. Raymond talked about his shop and lake house. Linda's Daddy talked about the real estate market and golfing.

It was time for the Barfield's to return home. They were happy and will pleased. Maria had nothing other than positive things to say about their trip. They both felt attached to Linda and her parents. Maria could hardly wait to share the news with her parents. They would both be so pleased that Jody was getting married and coming home. They drove on to Jo's and Paps' before they went home. Jo and Paps were anxiously waiting for them to come or call. Jo had thought they would be too tired to drop by, but she was waiting for the call.

Paps and Jo were mesmerized at the news of Jody getting married. Maria told them all about Linda and her family, and how she and Raymond felt toward them. Maria said, "Linda is a very beautiful girl.

She is a loving person, and she also sings. No wonder Jody fell for her."
Raymond agreed with her up to a point. He said Maria was the most
beautiful girl he'd ever seen. Maria said "You know that's not true." "O,
yes it is." Paps almost shouted. Jo glared at Paps and said, "I thought
I was." "You are when our daughter is not around." Then Paps said
he was so happy for Jody. He said that they would know next Sunday
whether or not Jody got the job. The issue had already been brought to
a vote, and the elders would make the announcement Sunday. Maria
and Raymond, both, were thinking; Paps already knows. The vote was
a yes. But he's not going to tell. Jo asked, "Do you know what furniture
Jody might need, and What about linens, dishes, and other things?"
Paps suggested that Jody and Linda make those decisions. Raymond
said "Let them decide, then we'll know what to get for wedding gifts."
All agreed.

The Barfields went home and went to bed. "Will we be able to go to
work in the morning?" Raymond asked. "If we get up in time, we will."
Maria answered. Neither one gave any thought to setting the clock to
alarm, which they usually did. They over slept for more than an hour.
Maria jumped up, jumped into her uniform, brushed her hair, and lift.
Raymond didn't have to be in any hurry. He didn't have to be on the
job at any particular time. He did, however, try to be there by eight.
He called his office, then fixed himself some breakfast. He got dressed
and to work only two hours late. When Maria got to the hospital, she
checked in, and got permission to go to the cafeteria for a few bites
before going on duty. She was still a bit tired.

At lunch the girls, as usual, wanted to know all about her trip.
They were awed at the surprise Maria had to face. "Why didn't Jody
tell you before you met the girl face to face? He could have told you
on the phone before you left." Maria answered, "I don't know." Dr.
Lopez was laughing at the girls. "We men don't have to tell you women
everything. As little as possible is enough." A loud voice answered. "I
absolutely agree with you." Amazed, everyone looked around and there
stood Raymond. "You're running late." Maria said. Dr Lopez replied,
"And look who's talking." He looked at Raymond and said, "She was
late for work this morning, and then had to take time out for breakfast.
Sometimes women can be a pain." Raymond laughed, "You got that
right." Maria announced, "Both of you guys can leave the table." "Sure

we can, but not before we're ready." Dr. Lopez informed her. After the fun lunch, they all departed. Raymond kissed Maria, while the others watched. He left without telling her what time he got to work.

Maria called Allison and told her the family news. Allison was so happy for Jody. She was sure Jody would invite her to his wedding, and she and Wallace would be there. She began to cry when Maria told her the church would announce the final decision Sunday. "I want Jody to get that position. He deserves it." Allison sobbed. "Be sure and let me know by Sunday afternoon." She pleaded. Allison said that she and Wallace were doing good, and were expecting a response soon on a job application Wallace had sent in a week ago. That uplifted Raymond when Maria told him. "Wait, Wait, That's all we can do now." Raymond said. Jody called to tell them he and Linda would be there Friday night. He had decided to be there for the vote results. Pastor Harris had called him and recommended that he be there. He had already spoken with the leadership team, and they were all positive. Maria rushed to tell Raymond, whose response was, "Remember what I said about waiting?" The whole family was waiting.

Maria got the bedroom fixed for Linda, and bought new linens for her bathroom. Surely, they would not go to Jody's house, except to look it over. Maria felt sure Linda would love the warm and friendly painted rooms. Raymond said he wanted to bring a new life to his house before Allison and Wallace moved into it. He wanted Maria to choose the colors. Raymond had a strong feeling that Allison would come home too. Maria suggested that they stop waiting for Jody, go on to the house and start painting. Out the door they went.

Raymond's house was in good shape, but Maria decided to re-paint the kitchen and dinning room. Then it occurred to her to wait before she bought the paint and let Allison choose the colors. Maria was busy getting her own house in order, planning meals, and enhancing the visitation. Paps and Jo were anxiously waiting to meet Linda. Jo, too, had some house cleaning to do before the expected arrival. Both Paps and Jo felt excited, but calm, about the news on the vote. Since Paps was Chairman of the Board of Elders, he would make the announcement. Whatever it turned out to be, Jo told Maria that she and Paps didn't know what to get for the wedding gifts. Maria told her, "I think you two have given him quiet enough already. A house and a lake house was enough."

Jody and Linda arrived late Friday night, but dinner was waiting for them. Maria showed Linda to her room. There, she hugged her and said, "I always wanted a daughter, and soon, I will have one. Jody met them in the kitchen, turned to Linda and said, "Remember what I told you, What ever she puts on the table is anybody's guess. Sometimes, she doesn't know what it is either. But your only choice is to eat it, go to bed and have stomach cramps." Maria threw a dishrag at him, and told him,"Get out of the kitchen, and don't come back until I call you. You don't have to come then." Linda stood in silence for a moment, then burst into laughter. Jody put his arms around her and said. "I told you." Raymond heard the emotions and came into the kitchen. He looked at Linda and said, "O. Lord, Mother and son are at it again." Linda was still laughing. Actually, Maria had prepared Jody's favorite meal, fried fish, cold slaw, and cheese grits. After the good time together, Jody rose from the table and said,

"Thanks Mom. Nobody could have fixed a better meal, except Linda." Linda said she and Jody would clean up the kitchen.

Saturday morning Jody and Linda picked up Jo and Paps, and they all went to the lake. Jody asked, "Paps, can I take your boat out:" Paps glared at him "It's not my boat. It's yours. So do as you please." Raymond said he and Maria would take her parents out on the boat with them. Jody questioned Raymond. "You're going fishing with her again?" Raymond said no way; he was merely going out for the ride. Jo and Paps were so glad to be out again. Jo had brought potato salad and fried chicken for lunch. She said to Jody, just before he and Linda took off, "Be back by twelve, so we can eat. Paps has to eat early." Jody took Linda to Paps' cabin, but explained to her that it was actually his. Linda liked the cabin, and had never been on a boat ride before. She enjoyed the voyage Jody took her on. She mostly loved the relationship Jody had with his mother.

Sunday morning sneaked in on them. Raymond knocked on Jody's door. Then opened it, and stuck his head in, "If you're going to church, you can't sleep all day." Jody jumped up. "Thanks, Dad." Maria had breakfast ready. She then tapped on Linda's door, but said nothing. Jody also tapped on Linda's door, and she got up. They were all a little excited as they went out the door, and then toward the church. The church was full. People they had not seen for a while were back. Jody was a bit nervous, but held Linda's hand. Pastor Harris came over to them and Jody made introductions. Before the service ended, Jody and Linda sang two hymns. The Pastor, then announced that Jody Marshall would be their new pastor in thirty days. Jody stood up as the Pastor introduced Linda to the crowd. He told the congregation that within thirty days, Jody would be married and move back home. Everyone applauded.

Time came for Jody and Linda to leave. Maria embraced them, and whispered to each, "I love you." Raymond did the same. Jody was most pleased that he had a job. Linda had picked up several real estate broachers to find out more about the area. She was very pleased with Jody's house that Paps had given him. She enjoyed Jody's Grandparents, and liked them both very much. Most of all, she really did like Raymond, and she loved Jody's mother. When they arrived home, Linda shared the visit with her parents. Though they hated to see her move, they were well pleased that she had connected with Jody, and that he was to be a minister. Jody and Linda began to make plans. Time was cutting them short. Number one was the wedding plans. They got the calendar out and began looking at dates. They found one!

Jody called to let them know the date. Maria needed more time, but time was running out. They would be married in eight days. Raymond and Maria would take her parents with them. Raymond called Allison, but she already knew and was making her plans to go. Jo was a bit upset about the short notice, but Paps explained. "Jody was only given a thirty day notice. That barely gave him time to set a wedding date, get married, move, and get settled in his new job." Jo calmed down, but wanted to know what gift Maria was giving. Maria had replaced some curtains and some bed spreads, plus painting the walls. She told her Mom that was her gift for the present time. Other things would surface later. She did not tell them that Raymond was giving Jody a thousand dollars. That was personal.

The day came, and the four left for Johnson City. Jody had made motel reservations for them. Allison and Wallace were in a room joining her parents. Allison was almost crying as she approached Raymond and Maria. Raymond asked her, "What's wrong?" She embraced him and said, "Nothing. I'm just so happy for my brother. I can't wait to meet Linda. Jody has nothing less than praise to say about her." "You will love her." Raymond said. Jody came by the motel for a short while. He would lead them to the church in the morning. He, too, was a bit shaky. He was very pleased that Allison and Wallace were there. He was most happy that his Grandparents were able to be there. Before he left, Raymond patted him on the back, and said, "Hold your self up, smile, sing, and be jolly. This is not the end of your life, it's the beginning. Happier days are ahead of you." Jody said, "Thanks Dad. I really needed that."

There was a good crowd at the church, and everyone was so friendly. Now, Maria was a bit shaky. Her own son, born a short time ago was getting married. Time flies, and she was barely aware that Jody was twenty three. Jo and Paps looked good. They both were really dressed up for this occasion. They must of felt a little of what she did. Their grandson was old enough to get married! Maria had to stop reminiscing, and come back to reality. Music had started, and Jody was standing up front with the Pastor. "Here Comes the Bride began to be played. The crowd rose to their feet. Maria glanced behind her, and was well rewarded. Linda was so beautiful holding to her Daddy's arm. The little girls dropping rose petals along the way were also beautiful. Maria's attention fell back on her son. He was a handsome man, she already knew. He had his eyes on Linda with a good smile on his face. Raymond was his Best Man, and Allison played the piano. Maria did not know the Bride Maids. It was soon over, and the reception was waiting.

Linda introduced each member of Jody's family to each member of her family. They met several family friends, all of whom spoke well of Linda's family. Many expressed their sorrow for loosing Jody, but gratitude that he was becoming a minister. The Pastor talked with Raymond and Paps about Jody's accomplishments. He was proud of Jody and wished him well. Maria was looking around for Jody. Jody and Linda were already gone. He didn't even tell her bye, or where he was going. She told Raymond. Raymond laughed at her, and again reminded her that she would no longer be number one. A man leaving on his honeymoon doesn't run to tell Mom. He was still laughing at her, She wanted to ask Linda's mother, but didn't. She did know that they were going to Myrtle Beach; at least Jody had mentioned it. But suppose they had a change of plan, and she didn't know where her son was, she kept moaning to Raymond. Raymond grabbed her into his arms, spanked her butt, and said, "Will you stop worrying about your little boy who is lost and no telling where. He's not alone. I don't know where he is, but I do know what he's doing. And poor little fellow has no one to instruct him. Perhaps, I should have gone with him." Maria grabbed a hand full of his hair and pulled it. Then she started laughing. They got Jo and Paps and hit the road.

Chapter 16

Allison and Wallace followed them home. Raymond helped Jo and Paps get into their house. Wallace carried their luggage in for them. Home at last, Maria felt good. She had accepted facts. She and Allison went to Jody's house. Allison had not seen the finished project, and wanted to. She liked the colors and the new curtains. They then, went to Raymond's house for Allison to decide if she wanted to paint a few walls. She did. She loved the grayish hues, and asked Maria to paint her kitchen and dinning room. She would also need a nursery. If her baby was a boy, she wanted the nursery blue. If it was a girl, she wanted it pink. Maria suggested they paint the walls beige, and use the colors for curtains, throw rugs, and other decorations. Allison agreed. So now, the project could began. Maria would get the nursery furniture also, that would be her gift. Raymond and Wallace came in as they were about to leave. Allison told Wallace their plan. He agreed.

As soon as Raymond and Maria were alone, Raymond said, "Let's sneak off to the lake." Maria's response was, "I'm too tired." Raymond said he was too, but needed a get away. On their way to the lake, Raymond suggested that they plan a trip very soon. They would take a week off and go camping. She suggested Myrtle Beach. Raymond suggested Niagara Falls. Raymond then said, "We will do both. If you don't have any bikinis, I'll get you a pair. She didn't have any, she told him. "But I do have some ragged underwear." "That will do." Raymond said. They greatly enjoyed their lake trip, and they both needed some time alone. Rippling waters are good therapy.

Jody and Linda started, that much too many chores, of moving into their house. Jody set up an office for himself, and one for Linda. She had a job and would start to work on the day that Jody did. Jody would spend much of his time in the church office, but would also need one at home. They had most of what they needed already in the house. Raymond had been working on the desk, but was not finished yet. As soon as they unpacked their luggage and put their clothes away, that was about all they had to do. There were enough furniture in the house, and surely enough kitchen appliances. As Raymond and Maria were helping them, Jody said the only thing they needed at the moment was groceries. He said they had given no thought to that. Raymond remarked, "Son, you'll soon learn that groceries are always at the top of the list."

Maria and Raymond had other things to do. Allison had called to tell them that Wallace got the job at a high school near them. Raymond knew exactly where it was located. Now, he began to feel better. Allison said they had already started packing, Raymond began thinking. Allison wouldn't need any furniture either. Most of his was still in the house. All of her mother's kitchen items were still there. Allison would, however, have a lot of unwanted items to dispose of. Raymond and Allison had already gotten rid of her mother's clothing, and some other things that neither of them wanted. Raymond and Maria had cleaned the house and rearranged some things.

They got a crib and a high chair for the nursery. As they left, Maria noticed that Raymond had a quivering voice.

Maria asked Raymond to wait until Allison had her baby before they went on their trip. There was enough to do in the meantime. Raymond said he had been thinking the same. Maria told him, "I want you to be here when that little girl calls for her grand paw." "And who told you it was a girl?" Raymond asked. Maria said, "No one. I just happen to know." Raymond offered, "I bet you ten dollars it's a boy." Maria accepted the offer, and they went to the River Walk for the rest of the evening. Raymond carried some maple flavored pop corn, and they each had a bottled drink. They sat at their favorite table, munched and sipped for two hours. They then took the walk and looked out over the river. Before they went home, they checked in on Maria's parents. All appeared to be well.

Maria picked up Jo and went to the studio. They had not painted together for a while. Jo had gone a couple of times without Maria. Maria had her hands full for a while. Maria told Jo, "As soon and Allison and Wallace move in, and the baby is born, that will free me and Raymond." Jo said, "Both of you have had a load lately." At the studio, they had other things to think about. They both needed some new paint and brushes. Maria bought a different illustration book for a view of varying designs and ideas. They both preferred oil over acrylics. But they both would choose acrylic over water color. They loved the way oils would blend. The class was to paint a bridge near a water fall. Maria thought of Niagara Falls and smiled. She wasn't ready to share that with her mom yet. They both thought the water fall would be easy, but feared the bridge. They soon changed their minds.

Jo and Paps dropped in on the Barfields, which surprised Maria. Her dad didn't drive, and her mom didn't drive at night. Jo was laughing. "I just had to show you this." She pulled a canvas from behind her to show Maria her waterfall. Maria started laughing. "Mom, it's suppose to be water falling from the mountain top, not to it." They all laughed. Jo said, "That's why I'm here. How do I make the water flow down instead of up?" Raymond looked at the canvas, and asked, "Is that water? It looks like snow balls to me. What do you think Paps?" Paps was amused, "Looks like white boards to me." Maria said, "Mom, your brush strokes are backwards, and you need a little more blue mixed with your white. Remember, blue and white are water colors."

At the next class Jo's waterfall looked much like what it was. Marias was not too pleased with her own, but the instructor pointed out her errors. Yet, Maria looked around, and decided her painting looked as real as anyone else's. There was something wrong with all of them. Then she came to her senses, that's why they were all in class, they were learning. Maria and Jo really enjoyed classes together. They would laugh at each others work, but never their own. As they reached the finish line, it was obvious that no two paintings looked exactly the same, but all looked somewhat realistic. The instructor claimed that she could not say which one, if any one, was best.

The phone rang before Maria and Raymond had gotten up.

Raymond took the call. It was Allison. They had moved into the house, and wanted to let them know. They had nothing to bring but personal items. Raymond asked them to come on down for breakfast. He then wondered if they had bought any groceries. Maria got up and got dressed. Raymond had gotten up and made coffee. He was fixing breakfast. When Allison and Wallace arrived, breakfast was on the table. They both were so pleased with the paint job, the crib and high chair. Allison loved the curtains. She embraced Maria, and then her dad. Wallace also showed appreciation. As Allison embraced Raymond, he said, "You are the prettiest little pregnant girl I ever saw." He held her close as tears dripped onto the top of her head.

No, they had not bought any groceries. Maria went shopping with Allison. Allison asked her to make a list of things she'd need. She didn't know what all to buy for an empty kitchen. She had not done much cooking since she and Wallace married. She didn't have time. They always ate breakfast on their way to work, and picked up something for dinner on their way home. She seldom made much more than sandwiches. Maria was thinking how things have changed. Today's working woman does not cook. Allison wouldn't be going back to work, so she would have time to fix some meals at home. Maria told her there was nothing greater than to sit down at a table with family and enjoy a meal together, no matter what it was. Allison would learn now that a family of her own was beginning to exist.

Wallace would be idle until September when school started back. He would work with Raymond until then. That would also give him time to do work at home. Time was running short for his child to be born. A couple more weeks and the lullaby tune would play for Maria. She and Raymond were both very excited. Marie started calling Raymond "grand paw." He told her to forget it, he would be called Papa, and Maria would be called Gigi. Maria asked. "Where did that come from? I never heard it." Raymond said, with his mouth open and pointing his finger to it, "It came from here." Maria thought about that and compared Gigi to other words she's heard. Yes, she liked Gigi. She then wondered what Allison would think about that. She told Allison what her dad had said. Allison had never heard it either, but she agreed, because, like Maria thought, it sounded good to her.

Maria told Jo. She wanted to know what the baby would call her.

They had fun trying to come up with something new. Maria asked Jo what she would want Jody's children to call her. "After all, they will be your great grands." Jo pondered for only a second. "Jojo" She said. Maria told Jody when he dropped by that evening. He thought Gigi and Jojo were very funny. He said he'd tell Linda. Maria and Raymond were both getting excited. It had been over twenty years since a new family member had been born. Raymond kept warning Maria to watch out, new members would surround them.

The phone rang in the middle of the night; Raymond grabbed it. "Dad, I'm on my way to the hospital, met me there." Maria was up and getting dressed before Raymond hung up he phone. She could tell by his voice, that time had come. Neither Maria nor Raymond were allowed into the delivery room. They waited and waited. The lullaby began, Maria grabbed Raymond's arm. "It's here." She almost screamed. Raymond knew too, what the lullaby meant. Wallace came to them, but couldn't think of what to say. Maria brought him out of his maze. "Wallace what is it?" Now looking normal, he said. "It's a girl and a boy." Raymond asked, "Can we see them?" Wallace said "Not yet." He then returned to be with Allison. Raymond was a bit impatient.

A nurse, who Maria knew, came and informed them."You can see your grand children now grand paw." Raymond jumped out of his chair. He looked at the nurse and said, "I am not grand paw, I am Papa." She led the way. Raymond and Maria followed. They saw Allison first. She was giggling. "Do you know we have twins, a girl and a boy? That's what we wanted." Raymond was concerned about Allison, but was feeling normal. Maria led him to the nursery. The twins were brought to the viewing window. Raymond never felt more elated. Which one was the boy, he couldn't tell. They looked too much alike. They were beautiful babies and looked like Allison, he concluded. Maria agreed with him, but they didn't tell Wallace.

Jody and Linda walked in to see Allison. Jody kissed her cheek. "Well I hear you did a great job. I haven't seen the twins yet, but I hear, from you know who, that they are the most beautiful babies ever born." Raymond was listening and smiled. Wallace was still with Allison, so Jody and Linda went to see the twins. Jody wondered what they would name them. "Maybe they'll name the boy after me." He told Linda. Her response was "I'm sure Wallace would love that." Linda told Raymond what Jody had said, and his response was, "When you have your first son, will he be named after me or you?" Jody said time would tell.

The twins were named Maria Allison and Raymond Wallace. Raymond couldn't keep his face dry. Maria was also deeply touched. By the time the twins came home, Maria had bought another crib. Wallace's parents were there, and stayed with Allison. They too, were too happy that the twins had arrived. They stayed a week with Allison and Wallace. Maria wondered how the other grand parents felt about the names, and of course, she already knew that Allison and her mother had the same name. Maria and Raymond went to say good bye to Wallace's parents, who would be leaving early in the morning. The twins were happily kicking.

Home at last, Raymond said, "Is there anything else we have to wait for? We have been waiting a long time." Maria said, "Do we have long to wait for out camping trip?" Raymond said, "No." Jody and Linda came by; they were on their way to see the twins. Raymond remarked, "I'm sure they were not planning for two." Jody told them that Allison knew she was caring twins. He goes on to say he and Linda will have quadruplets in a couple of years. Maria yelled, "Please don't." Linda said to Jody, "Then you have them, I'm not." "That will be the day." Raymond commented, then added, "Jody, if you ever go into labor, do not call your mom. She wouldn't know what to do. Call me."

Raymond and Maria planned their trip in detail. They would first go to Myrtle Beach for two days, then to Niagara Falls for four days, and get back home on the tenth day. They would make a few short stops on their way there and back. Maria shared their plan with her parents. Jo didn't approve their leaving until the twins were a little older. Maria informed her that the twins were not hers, nor her responsibility. Jody and Linda would be there if anyone was needed. Maria had already talked with Jody about the trip. He wanted them to go. He would look out for his grandparents and help Allison is she needed any help. Maria was a little hesitant about leaving her parents, but they would not be alone. Maria told Jody she would call every night while she was gone. Raymond asked Wallace to look after his business until he got back. Wallace already knew his way around, and would keep an eye on everything.

The beach offered a relaxation they both needed. It had been several years since either of them had been to the beach. The warm sand was a good massage to their bare feet, and the cool water added a new sensation to their bodies. They didn't do much swimming, but they did a lot of playing in the sand and shallow waters. Sun set was overwhelming for both of them. Never had they seen such beauty. The sun dipping down into the ocean and casting her rays to reflect on the waves. Maria shed a few tears. God is so awesome, she recalled. From the rocking chairs on the motel porch, they viewed the surround scenery most all night. Just before the sun came up, Raymond decided it was time to go to bed.

In the morning they strolled the beach, and did much wading in the water, as well as, getting a good walk. They walked bare-footed into the restaurant and ate breakfast. They couldn't eat for laughing. "When, if ever, have you walked into a restaurant bare-footed.?" Raymond asked Maria. "I don't remember." She responded. Back at the motel, they put their swim suites on and got back into the water. Maria picked up shells along the water's edge. She thought they were so pretty. Raymond wanted to know what her plan was. She told him to wait and see. He, too, became a little attracted to the different shaped shells, and begin picking up a few and putting them in his pocket. He asked Maria if she'd also like to take some sand home with her. She threw a shell at him.

Leaving the beach was no joy to either of them, but the ride to Niagara Falls would be a new and fun experience also. From the beach on, they would sleep in the camper. They had already lived through a beach sunset without walls around them. There could be nothing else more breath-taking, if as much. Their first stop was at a state park where they stayed overnight. They walked the area over and enjoyed a lunch. Back on the road, things got quiet. Maria had been playing her favorite music and singing, but not now. Raymond glanced at her, "What are you doing?" She looked up at him, "I'm trying to find out something about Niagara Falls. I got some information, but never looked at it." Raymond's response was, "Keep your eyes on the road, and look for a place to stop. Tonight, we'll read about Niagara Falls." Maria got her music started again.

They camped at another state park where someone was cooking out. The whole area was covered in a light smoke that caused Raymond to pull into the camp ground. "Someone is grilling out. I hope they'll invite us to dinner." As soon as they got settled in their camp site, they got out of the camper and started wondering around. Raymond let Maria toward the smoking grill. "Smells good." He said. "I've got enough for two more. Come join us." Raymond came to a stand still.

"Thank you. I think we will." Maria was embarrassed, to say the least. She gave Raymond a disgusting look. Introductions were made. They were extremely friendly people. "You can help me get the drinks." The lady said to Maria.

When they got back into their camper for a good night's sleep, Maria said to Raymond, "Don't you ever do that again." Raymond knew he had embarrassed her, buy why? He turned to her and said, "Maria that's part of what camping is all about. Campers mix and mangle. They talk about their lives: who they are, where they came from, where they are going, how many children they have, and what kind of work do they do. That's what I like about camping." Maria embraced him, kissed him, and said she was sorry. The next morning, Raymond made hot cakes, and invited their neighbors for breakfast. They accepted.

Their next over night stop was in Harrisburg, one they would never forget. They were most excited over the Sesquehanna River that is a mile wide at Harrisburg, but is not navigable. Harrisburg on the east side of the Sesquehanna, is easy accessible. They drove through Capitol Park, in the heart of the city, and visited the State Museum. They found that Harrisburg had many large state parks. River Park extends five miles along the river. The municipal bathing beach and baseball park occupy an island, reached by two bridges in the middle of the Sesquehanna.

Happily, they arrived in Buffalo, the second largest city in New York, and connected to Canada by the Peace Bridge and International Bridge. They visited the Museum of Science. Maria loved browsing through museums, no matter what kind they were. Raymond was more interested in water fronts, piers, and docks. Surrounded by Lake Eric and Lake Ontario, Buffalo was a perfect place for them to be. They found a breath taking camp site and stayed there overnight. Maria made coffee and pored each of them a bowl of cereal for breakfast. Raymond wasn't particularly fond of cereal, but ate it. He then fixed himself a pop tart.

Niagara Falls was a site to behold. From the Canadian side, the falls were awesome. Great tourist attraction, luring millions of visitors each year, is a great asset to their economy. Maria and Raymond drove around looking over the area. They learned that more than half of Ontario is a low, rocky plateau with many lakes. Ontario is a major industrial center. They visited one of Maria's favorite stops, the Niagara Falls Museum, with collections of art and historical materials. Neither Raymond nor Maria were aware of the two waterfalls separated by Goat Island, New York. They took the boat ride to the back side of the falls. And afterwards, they toured the gardens. It was the most beautiful flowers they had ever seen. Raymond asked Maria if she'd like to take a bouquet home with her. She said, "No. We would probably end up in jail if we pulled one bloom." Before they left, they sat down on a bench right in front of the falls, and watched it for an hour. How fascination it was! Again, Maria proclaimed, "God is awesome." She took several pictures, and they left.

They found a restaurant on Lake Erie, and stopped there. Most of the walls were glass, and the view encouraged them to enjoy the meal. Raymond said they should look over Buffalo before they left, just in case they decide to move there. Maria corrected him. She said they would be moving to Harrisburg. Raymond shook his head. They spend a couple of hours looking around Buffalo where they were most interested in lakes. They drove on to Rochester, and then headed south.

Maria called Jody, and all was well there. He had a full house at church on Sunday, and two new members joined the church and were baptized. He said his goal was to bring in more young members, and he was aiming at that. Linda would be working on a larger choir. He said he picked up his grandparents and took them to church, then to lunch, and then home. Linda had two listings to sell a house, and one prospective buyer. She had a good week. Maria shared the information with Raymond. He said Linda could sell their house, and find them one in Buffalo. But Marie argued that they could not sell their house, because they would need a place o stay when they visited the children. They could not stay with the children, because their houses would be full of screaming grand children. Raymond said, "O.K. You are right again. I certainly don't want to stay in a house full of screaming kids." It was time for a break. Raymond had been driving all day and was ready to stop. Maria heated some canned meat and vegetables. She then opened a can of peaches. It didn't look too good, but they were too tired to look for a restaurant. They ate every bite, took a shower, and then watched a movie that Maria had bought at one of the museums they had toured. When the movie ended, the lights went off, and they went to bed. Raymond told Maria to walk softly when she got up in the morning, for he didn't plan to make and foot steps before nine o'clock.

Their first stop that day was Ashville. They had heard of the place, but knew nothing about it. They looked over a public library in search for tourist attractions. The Biltmore House appeared to be number one to Maria. Raymond wanted to look into the Blue Ridge Mountain area. The Blue Ridge Parkway, averaging three thousand feet above sea level, follows the Blur Ridge through Virginia and North Carolina for more than four hundred miles. Ashville is on a plateau between the Blue Ridge and Smoky mountains. The city is particularly noted as a health and a vacation resort. Near by is the Great Smoky Mountains National Park.

After containing the necessary information, they went for a ride. Maria was scared speechless as the road made sharp turns to the right, then to the left. It the road wasn't running in semi circles, it was running straight up or straight down. She had a great fear of the camper going on a roll. Raymond said finally, "This would certainly be a bad place for the brakes to go bad." Maria almost started crying. She made no comment. Raymond again commented. "If I ever find a place to pull off, I will." His dream came true. Around the next circle, was a road-side parking area. Raymond pulled over and parked. Then, as they began to look around, they decided the ride was worth it. Never had they seen such high mountains. Raymond told Maria, "Look down in the valley and you'll realize how high up we drove." She loved the valley, but did that mean they would have to drive straight down to get out of the mountains. Surely, they would flip over head first on their way out. She asked Raymond if he was afraid while driving. He said, "I was a bit shaky a couple of times."

A wide stream bubbling over massive rocks got their attention. Other people were out on the rocks, and for them to do the same, appeared to be the ideal thing to do. They took their shoes off, and climbed down into the stream. Raymond found a rock high enough to sit on, and he did with his feet swaying in the cool waters. That looked relaxing to Maria, and she did the same thing. They swung their legs to and fro, talked and laughed. Soon they were both calm. There were others near them, and conversation broke loose. They found out about some other travelers: who they were, where they were from, and where they were going. After more time than they had expected, Raymond wanted to get back on track before night-time caught him in the valley. They left, but not without looking back.

It was more dangerous getting out of the mountains, than getting into them, Raymond concluded. It was, they both agreed, the most interesting views they'd seen. To be in the valley looking up, or on the mountain looking down, was Raymond's greatest pleasure. The views were not explainable. There were no words to actually describe it. Maria, too, was caught up in the great wonders that any such landscape could exist. "God, how did you do it?" she whispered. They had no trouble getting back on level ground. Both of them pondered if they'd ever do it again. "Certainly not in the camper." Raymond told Maria. "A number of times, I thought it swayed a bit." Maria said, "But wouldn't a lighter weight vehicle be more apt to sway?" Raymond replied, "I'll never know."

Chapter 17

Raymond wanted to stop at the lake house on the way home, stay a day and night, and then go home not so tired. They got there around sun-down, fixed a snack and sat on the porch until dark. They went to bed and slept all night. Raymond made some pancakes and fried some bacon; he then, woke up Maria. "Your breakfast is ready dear one." She got up dragging her feet. They sat at the table and enjoyed their meal. The coffee was what Maria needed since she had a light head ache. She usually felt better after her coffee. As soon as they had eaten they went back to bed. Raymond held her close telling her what a great person she was. He said "My life has never been so great as it's been with you." She responded, "I really never had a life until I got you." They both went to sleep.

Someone knocked on the door, Raymond jumped up. It was Jody. "I saw the camper here, and decided to give you a call," he said. "Sorry I woke you up. It's only two o'clock." Maria came into the room. Jody said, "Good afternoon sleepy head. They couldn't believe it was two o'clock. "What are you doing here?" Maria asked. Jody said he and Linda had just got there. They decided to stay a day and night at his lake house. Linda entered the room. "I got tired of waiting for you." she said to Jody. Maria embraced both of them, and asked about the rest of the family. "All is well." Linda said. They talked briefly about their trip and offered to fix a snack, but Jody said, "No." Jo then turned to Linda, "Let's go and let these two old people go back to bed. They'll probably sleep for two or three more days." He laughed. Maria answered, "I wish we could." The four went out on the boat and drifted until a huge fish flounced around near them. Raymond got his fishing pole ready and threw it in. Jody joined him. The women just set back, talked, and enjoyed the breeze. Raymond caught four fish and Jody caught four. They went back to the dock and the Barfields left for home. Raymond gave his fish to Jody, "You clean them and eat them."

Raymond and Maria stopped by her parents before going home. They were having dinner, so the four sat at the table together, and had a great visit. Jo told Maria that Paps didn't feel good. He was tired, though he had not done anything. Jo felt fine. They talked about their trip and answered a hundred questions. Raymond told them that he and Maria were moving to Buffalo. Maria cut him off, and said they would move to Harrisburg. Paps cut her off, "No, you're not. You're staying right where you are. Understand?" They both bowed to him and said, "Yes sir."

As they entered their own house, Raymond grabbed Maria, swirled her round, and said, "The best part of any vacation is getting back home. She agreed. "There's no place like home." Raymond called Allison to check on them. She said the twins were doing good. Wallace had not got home yet, but had a good ten days managing Raymond's business. She warned her Dad to be careful that Wallace didn't take over the business. He liked it that much. Raymond told Maria to go to bed; he was going to drop by on Allison for a short visit. "So am I." she answered. They both went. The twins were so precious. They were now smiling and throwing their hands up toward them. Allison did have both hands full, but she said they were very quiet as long as she was in the room with them. So, she sat in the rocker and read most of the time. When Wallace came home, he'd sit with them to give her a break. Back at home, the Barfields went to bed.

"The worse thing about a vacation is having to go back to work." Raymond said. "I've been thinking that too." Maria responded. Maria cooked bacon and eggs. They ate, got dressed, and went out the door. Now, Maria felt a little more pleased to be back on the job, and so did Raymond. The girls were glad to have Maria back. Dr. Lopez patted her on the shoulder, and said. "It's about time you go to work." Things had gone well for Raymond's business. Wallace had a couple of new contracts. New customers are a great asset.

That night Maria and Raymond prepared dinner for the whole clan- all ten of them. Maria threw a blanket on the dinning room floor for the twins. Raymond threw a couple of pillows onto the blanket. Now the twins would not be alone. Jody picked up his grandparents. Linda and Allison helped with the kitchen work. They baked a ham, sweet potatoes, and cooked some green beans. Linda made a banana pudding. "When we women get together, we show those guys what we can do." Maria said. "Watch them eat as if they were starving." Allison said. It was Linda's turn. "Jody will eat all he can hold, then make some remark about the food." They all laughed and agreed with her. Jo said, "Let's give the men some credit, after all, who's taking care of the babies?" Jody yelled out from the dinning room, "Thank you Granny."

Dinner was placed on the table that only sits eight people. How lucky she was, Maria thought. At least for now, the twins could stay on the floor. Jody told them that Allison was trying to get some teenagers into the church. She had talked with some teachers she knew, and had made contact with a long list of students that she had taught. Linda would assist her, as she looked into some younger choir members. Paps told them that Jody and Linda were handling the responsibilities of the church very well. He said the whole congregation was well pleased with them. Linda said the church needed a secretary, and she would take care of that on a part time basis, and keep her realtor job, for the time being. Paps approved of that. That would give Jody some free time to visit and mix with the members. Wallace said he'd soon be back on the job and would encourage the students to get involved in the church, at least those who never attended any church.

There was nothing left on the table but dirty dishes. Jo said, "O.K. you men clean up the kitchen while we women play on the blanket. Paps laughed and said. "You're still full of it, aren't you?" Raymond got up and said, "You boys follow me, and you women get out of our way." "Thank You." All of the women said. And, as Jo had said, the women got down on the level of the twins. As soon as the men finished the kitchen, it was time for everyone to leave. After the house emptied out, Raymond and Maria went out on the porch and rocked. They both said it was a great family time together. Maria remarked that they only had eight dinning chairs, and only eight to fill them. She would do this again very soon. But it never happened.

Maria was already dressed the next morning when the phone rang. It was Jo. She had called an ambulance to come get Paps. "Meet me at the hospital." She said. Maria called Jody and told him. Her and Raymond went to Jo's first. They got there about the time the ambulance did. Jo was calm, and asked them not to go into his room. Maria didn't like that at all. She said to Raymond "She thinks he's dead." Raymond said "Could be." Jo led the paramedics into the bed room and closed the door behind them. In a short while, they came out with Paps laying flat on his back, with a sheet over his body. Maria knew. They followed the ambulance to the hospital, and then waited in the E.R. They were called into another room, and told that Paps was dead. Jody could not control himself. Raymond grabbed him and held him close. Maria and Jo were embraced. Jody finally got control of himself and took over. They stayed with Paps until the undertakers arrived. Jody drove Jo and Maria where they all met.

Jo spent the night with Maria. Jo had asked Jody if he would be emotional able to preach the funeral. He said he was planning on it. The family met at Maria's the next morning, and before they left, Jody had a prayer. He prayed for strength and courage for each family member. Linda silently prayed for Jody. He would surely need strength and courage too. They all left together. Allison had already made arrangements for a baby sitter. The church was full when they arrived. Paps was already there. That is what they had waited for. Jody shook hands with a few friends. Everyone was seated. Allison began playing the piano. She played Paps' favorite hymn, Farther Along.

Jody took his position, standing behind the coffin. He looked down at Paps, smiled, and began. "As long as I have known my Grandfather, he's been on the road home. Now, he has finally arrived. He didn't just die, nor pass a way, and he is not gone. He moved from his home on earth to a mansion, the one that is already prepared for him. We had all rather live in a mansion than the shacks we're living in. We can all make the move, eventually, if we are on the road home. I hope you are, but if you are not, it's easy. Ask God to forgive your sins; he will, and then you too are on the road home. But once on the road, you must stay on it. Yes, there are some rocky places on the road. You must be as determined as Paps was to stay on it. He finally arrived, and believe me, it's worth the hassle. Raise your hand, if you think you're on the road home. Now raise your hand if you know you're on the road home.

After the burial, lunch was served at the church, and the family stayed and ate with friends. Jo was calm, which surprised everyone. She told a friend that she had been preparing for this a long time. She too, had prayed for strength and courage. Allison and Wallace had to take the twins home. They were getting a bit fussy. Jody stayed close to his mother, who was not too strong right now. Everyone praised Jody for the great job he did. Linda kept an arm around Jo. Raymond wondered around the crowd, enjoying small talk with several other men. Linda told Marie that Jo wanted to go home. Maria went to her mother and asked her to go home with her and Raymond for a couple of days. Jo agreed. Jody and Linda came by that night and stayed a while. Jo said to Jody, "I was so proud of you this morning. I know Paps would have loved it. You're right; he was on the road home a long time before he got there." Jody's reply was, "but thank God, he did."

Maria went to work the next morning. Jody and Linda stayed with Jo. Maria thanked the girls and Dr. Lopez for attending her Dad's funeral. They all said how surprised, as well as pleased, they were at Jody's presentation. They chatted until the bell rang, then they all got to their feet. Dr. Lopez asked Maria if she needed the day off. She said, "No." When she got into the cafeteria for lunch, she heard a familiar whistle. She looked around, and saw Jody, Linda, Raymond, and Jo. She was so pleased. Before they had finished eating, Maria was called to the birthing center, and away she went. Before long the lullaby rang loud and clear. The rest of the family left. Jo went home with Jody and Linda.

Linda had been quiet busy, but had plenty of time at home. She did much of her work at home. She had learned the area well and the surrounding areas well. Her greatest quality was her honesty and truth. If a house needed a new roof, or if the yard held water, she would share that with a prospective buyer. It might cost her a sale, but that didn't bother her. More than anything, she would be fair with her customers. And she was.

Jody liked to tell about an experience he and Linda had: On her way home one evening, Linda noticed an elderly lady on her knees, pulling weeds from her flower bed. The lady reminded her of Jo. Linda drove on home, changed clothes, and came back. She pulled into the driveway and parked her car. As she approached the lady, she said, "Good evening, my name is Linda, and I stopped by to help you." The old lady, said, "Thank you." She attempted to get up, but couldn't. Linda helped her up and led her to the doorsteps, where the lady sat down. Linda began pulling up weeds. It took her more than two hours to pull every weed. The flower bed was about three feet wide, and ran along the side of the house. When Linda finished, she helped the lady into her house. Backing out of the driveway, Linda ran into the mailbox and knocked it down. She went back and told the lady what she had done. "Don't worry about it," she said. "My husband will come and fix it." Linda left. She told Jody what happened and he immediately went and put up a new post and fixed the mailbox.

The lady said she had never known a person as kind as Linda. She asked Jody what he did for a living. She then asked if Linda worked, Jody told her that Linda was a realtor. The lady, then, wanted to know how she could get in touch with Linda. Jody gave her the information. When Jody got back home, he began teasing Linda, and told her not to knock down anymore mailboxes. Linda asked if he knew the lady's name. He didn't. Maria soon learned. The call came three weeks later. Mrs. Rambo wanted Linda to drop by for a chat. Linda stopped by the next morning.

Mrs. Rambo wanted to sell her house, and buy a condo. She wanted two bed rooms, and no yard. Linda took her to look at some condos. Mrs. Rambo chose one and bought it. Jody and Linda moved her into the condo. She told Linda that her sister wanted to make the same move. Linda went to her sister's, took her to Mrs. Rambo's, and the sister bought the condo next door. She then listed her house. Linda sold the two houses and another condo to Mrs. Rambo's friend. That gave Linda a great boost. She and Jody, so many times, talked and laughed about the way pulling weeds really paid off. Many times after that, when Linda was doing nothing, Jody would ask, "Isn't it about time you start pulling more weeds?" She'd laugh. That's the kind of person Linda was, always willing to help anyone who needed help. And she was rewarded.

Easter arrived, a bit early for Jo, but met everyone else's expectations. A family trip was pre-planed to the lake, where each of them found their own pleasure. Sure they all loved being in the boat and idlely drifting, but some loved to fish. Others loved to set on the dock, while some liked just browsing around the area. On this trip some would, for the first time, hunt for colored eggs. Linda's parents had come, and Wallace's parents were there. With two cabins and a camper, there was plenty of sleeping room for everyone. Jody whispered to his Mom that Linda was pregnant. She told Raymond. Maria giggled all day. Wallace wanted to take the twins out on the boat, but Allison was a bit hesitant. Linda went with them and held one of the twins. Jody enjoyed the site. For the evening prayer, before dinner, Jody said, "How grateful we are Lord for our families. Without them, what would life be? We're grateful too for the additions you hand to us. Occasionally we lose a member, but you replace them. Bless each of us, and help us to stay on the road home. Amen."

www.ingramcontent.com/pod-product-compliance
Lightning Source LLC
Chambersburg PA
CBHW051427280526
45785CB00003B/1187